Kindergarten Themes

Written by Mary J. Kurth
Edited by Vicky Shiotsu
Illustrated by Diane Kidd
Project Manager: Sue Lewis
Project Director: Carolea Williams

Table of Contents

To the Teacher

Kindergarten Themes contains eight thematic units filled with hands-on learning activities designed specifically for kindergarten children. Each unit is based on a child-oriented theme that will delight and intrigue young learners. The activities described in this resource book will help you develop your students' skills in a variety of curriculum areas as you invite the children to explore bugs, dinosaurs, and other motivating topics.

Creating a Theme-Centered Classroom

The thematic units in this book provide numerous ideas for encouraging children to investigate themes individually, in small groups, or with the whole class. Each unit includes the following:

Suggestions for Setting Up an Exploration Corner

The Exploration Corner is an independent learning center designed to allow students to explore and make discoveries on their own. Each time you begin a thematic study, introduce the topic by bringing your class to the Exploration Corner and describing the materials and activities that are available there. Suggestions for setting up the corner and descriptions of specific activities for the center are presented at the beginning of each unit. If possible, enlist the aid of students and parents in collecting inexpensive materials for the Exploration Corner. A Parent Letter is included on page 7; the letter informs parents about the theme your class is studying and lists some items you'll need to enrich your students' learning. If you wish, reproduce copies of the letter and send one home with each student.

A Theme-Related Literature List

A literature list of theme-related books accompanies each unit. These books are ideal for introducing a theme or for extending a specific topic of study. Share these books by reading the stories to your class or by placing them in the Exploration Corner for children to look at by themselves.

Hands-on Activities

Each thematic unit contains a wide variety of hands-on activities that incorporate different areas of the curriculum. Many of the activities can be set up in the Exploration Corner for students to do on their own or in small groups. Other activities may be done with all the students at one time for a whole-class learning experience.

Reproducible Pages

Each unit contains reproducible pages of patterns or pictures to be used with individual projects. A Multipurpose Page also is included at the back of each unit. Use these pages in a variety of ways:

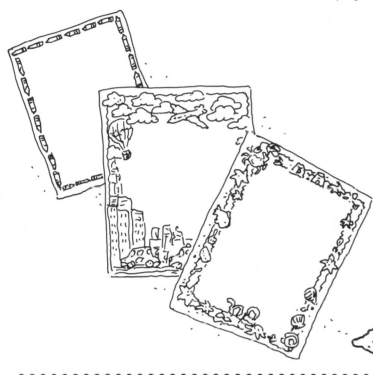

- Write a newsletter for parents informing them of classroom happenings.

- Create an achievement award for students who complete a unit of study. Write an appropriate statement in the center of the page, reproduce the page, and add a sticker.

- Let students use this page to practice writing and drawing skills.

- Write a thank-you note to students and parents who donated materials for your theme study.

Management Ideas

How long you spend on a unit depends on your goals and objectives. A period of two or three weeks is usually adequate for kindergartners. However, because children's interest levels vary, you may decide to continue a thematic unit for a month or more.

Begin gathering materials for each thematic study early and place the items you gather in large boxes or plastic containers that are easily accessible. You may want to use theme-related contact paper or rubber stamps to decorate the boxes and containers. Store papers, parent letters, and reproducible pages in file folders that are marked with the particular topic of study. Keep a bibliography of songs, books, and tapes that you plan to use with each theme; the bibliography will be a handy list you can refer to each year when planning a similar unit of study for a new class.

Team up with another teacher to share ideas and resources. Involve professional peers such as the school curriculum coordinator, librarian, and teachers who specialize in art, music, or physical education. Encourage parents to become actively involved by helping in the classroom with the various activities. This will allow you to break up the class into small groups and give more individual attention to each student.

Record-Keeping Tips

Evaluation and assessment of each student's progress should be ongoing. Assess student growth by observing children and writing notes about their participation in the various activities. Observe how children learn and interact with materials and with classmates. If you like, take pictures of individual children working on projects and then post the photos on a bulletin board. The pictures will delight your class, but they will also serve as a valuable record of what the students have done during their unit of study.

You can also make student portfolios to keep track of each child's progress. Simply print each child's name at the top of a file folder or accordion folder. Invite students to decorate their portfolios with drawings and photographs. Then store the portfolios in a convenient location. As students work through their theme study, fill the portfolios with samples of work that represent the children's various achievements. The portfolios are ideal for storing worksheets, stories, artwork, and other projects. Let each student make a new portfolio for each theme or have them make just one for the entire year. Later, let students look through their portfolios to see a running record of their accomplishments. Show the portfolios to parents, too, to give them an idea of their children's growth.

Kindergarten Themes is the perfect supplement to any kindergarten program. Each of the thematic units is built on the premise that young children learn best through hands-on experiences with concrete objects. As students become more actively involved in the learning process, they will experience a wonderful sense of discovery and self-confidence. These experiences, in turn, will foster a love of learning that will last children a lifetime.

Date _____

Dear Parents,

Our class is about to begin a theme study on _____.

We can't wait to learn all about the topic! Our class will be involved in theme-related activities that integrate language arts, math, and other areas of the curriculum.

The theme study will include an Exploration Corner—a learning center filled with materials that allow children to explore topics on their own. Whenever possible, we encourage children to bring toys, books, or other items that relate to our theme. Students enjoy sharing their own things with the class and having the items displayed in the Exploration Corner. If your child is planning to bring something to share, please talk about its characteristics with your child beforehand so that he or she will be able to discuss the item with the class. Please label each item with your child's name.

If you would like to donate an item to the Exploration Corner, it would be greatly appreciated! Here are some things we could use: toys, books, pictures, magazines, rubber stamps, stickers, fabric pieces, wrapping paper, costumes. We also need a few consumable items for our theme study. If you are willing to send an inexpensive item, please fill out the bottom portion of this form and return it to school. I will let you know the item we need and the date we will need it.

We look forward to exciting learning experiences as we begin our theme study! In the near future, your child will be bringing home some samples of what he or she has been doing in class. Please be sure to ask your child to tell you about them.

Sincerely,

_____

· ·

Yes, I can donate _____ for your upcoming theme study.

Or, just let me know what you need and the date you will need it.

Signed_____

Sand and Sea

Immerse your class in a fun-filled learning environment with the ideas in this unit. Your students will relax at the "beach," practice writing in a tub of sand, fish for magnetic letters, and more!

Exploration Corner

Create a Sand and Sea Exploration Corner that makes children feel as if they were at the seaside! Here are some ideas for setting up the corner:

- Cover a bulletin board with blue cellophane paper and add pictures of sea creatures.
- Cut out two paper outlines of children and tack the shapes onto a wall. Glue a colorful swimsuit to each shape. Let your students make paper fish to add to the display.
- Hang green crepe paper from the ceiling for seaweed.
- Place theme-related books in a small swimming pool. Add some comfortable pillows (in sand and sea colors, if possible) to create a comfortable reading area. Or, place books in a beach bag and store some beach towels in a box. Let the children spread out the beach towels and lie on them when they want to read.
- Cover a table with a shower curtain or a paper tablecloth that has an underwater theme, and set pencils, markers, scissors, and paper on the table to make a colorful work area.

Suggested Activities for the Exploration Corner

During your Sand and Sea theme study, set out some activities at the Exploration Corner that children can do independently. Use these ideas as springboards for your own creative activities:

- Put interesting objects (such as shells, pieces of coral, driftwood, and pebbles) in a box for students to examine with a magnifying glass.
- Fill a box with fishing gear, fishing boots, a fishing hat, goggles, flippers, sunglasses, a beach hat, a beach bag, and other theme-related costumes and props. Then let the children pull out the items and have fun dressing up.
- Fill a large plastic tub with sand. Set out small cups, shells, cookie cutters, and other items. Have the children press one item at a time into the sand to make imprints.
- Place a variety of theme-related activities on a shelf or table for children to do independently—jigsaw puzzles, stencils, rubber stamps, dot-to-dot puzzles, and so on.
- Make picture cards by attaching stickers of sea creatures and shells to index cards. Let the students use the cards for playing Concentration or Go Fish.

Books to Share

Here are some books that will enhance the Sand and Sea theme.

At the Seashore by David Schwartz (Creative Teaching Press)

Fish Eyes by Lois Ehlert

Follow the Water from Brook to Ocean by Arthur Dorros

House for Hermit Crab by Eric Carle

The Ocean Alphabet Book by Jerry Pallotta

Rainbow Fish by Marcus Pfister

Swimmy by Leo Lionni

Under the Sea: A First Look by Claire Llewellyn

The Underwater Alphabet Book by Jerry Pallotta

Water by Frank Asch

What's Under the Ocean? by Janet Craig

Activities

Sand Writing

Letter Recognition, Handwriting

Place a tub of wet sand on a table that's been covered with newspaper. Place a container of letter cards nearby. Each card should display one uppercase or lowercase letter.

Invite one group of students at a time to practice writing letters in the sand. Instruct each child to choose a letter card and use his or her finger to form the letter. The letters can be erased by running the edge of a plastic shovel across the sand.

Extension:

- Let each student practice writing his or her name in the sand.

- Provide word cards (add a picture of the word on each card when applicable) and let students practice writing the words in the sand.

Beach Ball Toss

Alphabet Sequencing, Large-Motor Skills

Have your students stand in a circle around you. Say the letter *a* and toss a beach ball to a student. The child who catches the ball must call out *b* and toss the ball back to you. Next, call out *c* and then toss the ball to another student. That child then calls out *d* and throws the ball back to you. Continue the procedure until the whole alphabet has been recited.

Variations:

- Call out numbers in order instead of letters.

- Call out a letter and toss the ball to a student. That child must say a word that begins with that letter before throwing the ball back to you.

- Say a word that relates to your theme study, such as *sand*, *beach*, or *water*. Throw the ball to a student. That child must say the letter that begins the word you called.

Stamping Fun
Visual Perception, Letter/Word Recognition

Reproduce the pictures on page 18, and cut out the animals. Glue each picture onto a piece of construction paper. Write the name of the picture on each paper, and display the pictures on a table or along the edge of a chalkboard.

Reproduce the Sand and Sea multipurpose page (page 19) so that each child has a copy. Then have the students choose one animal at a time and use rubber stamps to stamp the animal's name on their page. Have them draw pictures to accompany their stamped words. Challenge the children to read the words to you or to a friend.

Let's Go Fishing
Letter Identification, Fine-Motor Skills

Materials
- ✓ long wooden dowel or yardstick
- ✓ string
- ✓ magnet
- ✓ magnetic letters
- ✓ butcher paper
- ✓ scissors
- ✓ stapler
- ✓ large cardboard box (big enough for a child to sit in)
- ✓ metal surface such as a cookie sheet (optional)
- ✓ alphabet chart

Create a simple boat by cutting two large crescent shapes from butcher paper and stapling each shape to one side of a box. Make a magnetic fishing pole by tying a string to a dowel or yardstick and attaching a magnet to the end of the string. Have two students scatter the magnetic letters on the floor around the boat. One child then sits in the boat and fishes for the letters while the other child helps hook the letters onto the pole. The first child must say the name of each letter as it is pulled into the boat. After half the letters have been pulled in, have the children trade places. When all the letters have been caught, have both students arrange the letters in alphabetical order on a metal surface or on a table. (Post an alphabet chart nearby for reference.) Or, let the children take turns picking up a letter and naming an object that begins with that letter.

All Kinds of Fish

Science, Art, Creative Writing

Show your class pictures of different kinds of fish. Discuss what features fish have in common, such as fins, tails, and gills. Also talk about the ways in which fish differ. (They vary in color, size, and shape. Some, like the swordfish and the stingray, have unusual features.)

Later, have the class paint pictures of different kinds of fish. Then have each child dictate a sentence about their fish while you write it on a strip of paper. Display the pictures and the sentences on a bulletin board.

Underwater Scenes

Vocabulary Development, Art

Materials

- ✓ blue water wash (1 c. of water to 1 tbsp. of blue paint)
- ✓ paintbrushes
- ✓ crayon or oil crayon
- ✓ drawing paper (1 sheet per student)
- ✓ glue/water mix (2 tbsp. glue to 1/4 c. water)
- ✓ 2 cups of dry sand or bird grit (available at pet supply shops)

Share books with your class that depict life under the sea. Discuss the pictures and make a chart listing the different kinds of ocean life. Then have the class create their own underwater scenes. Instruct the children to draw their scenes with crayons and then cover the papers with the blue water wash. When the paint dries, have the students dab the glue mixture along the bottom of their papers and sprinkle on sand. Display the pictures when dry.

What Am I?

Critical Thinking

Cut out the pictures on page 18.
Then glue each picture on a sheet of construction paper. Display the pictures in a pocket chart or along the edge of the chalkboard.
Have the students take turns standing in front of the class and saying a riddle about one of the pictures.

Example: *I have eight legs.*
            I swim in the ocean.
            What am I?

Have the class guess the answer to each riddle.

Do They Live in the Sea?

Classification

Materials
✓ pocket chart
✓ beach bag
✓ 2 paper strips
✓ markers
✓ pictures of land animals and sea creatures

Put the words *Yes* and *No* in the pocket chart to make two columns. Place all the pictures in the beach bag. Have one student pull out a picture from the bag. Ask the child whether the picture is of a creature that lives in the sea. Have the child place the picture in the correct column on the chart. Continue the procedure with other students and pictures.

Shell Search

Number Recognition, Sequencing

Get 20 shells. Use a permanent marker to print a number from 1 to 20 on each shell. Bury the shells in a plastic tub half full of sand. Challenge your students to work individually or with a partner to search for the buried shells. As the shells are found, have the students say the number aloud. When all the shells have been found, have the children arrange the shells in order from 1 to 20. After their work has been checked by you or a classmate, let them hide the shells for other students to find.

Variations:

- Tell students to sequence the numbers backwards from 20 to 1.
- Get 26 shells. Print the letters from *a* to *z* on the shells. Have the students find the shells and put them in letter order.
- Write simple equations on one half of the shells and the answers on the other half. Have the students match the equations with the answers.

Aquarium Gravel Pit

Estimation, Measuring Volume

Label five containers of different sizes *A*, *B*, *C*, *D*, and *E*. Draw the outlines of five jars on a sheet of paper. Label the jars from *A* to *E*. Reproduce the page for each child.

Work with a small group of children at a time. Get scoops that are the same size and a tub of aquarium gravel. Place one scoop and container *A* in the gravel. Ask the students to estimate how many scoops it will take to fill the container. Then have the students use the scoops to fill the container. Have them record on their paper the number of scoops they needed to fill jar *A*. Have the students continue the procedure with the other jars. Later, ask the children if they were able to estimate more accurately the more times they measured.

Sand-Filled Weights

Estimation, Measuring Weight

Materials

- ✓ 3 or more plastic containers of different sizes (such as food containers and toy bowls)
- ✓ tub of sand
- ✓ sand shovel or scoop
- ✓ balance scale

Show the students how to use the scale. Tell them that we know a truck is heavier than a feather without using a scale. Explain that a balance scale lets us figure out which objects are heavier or lighter when the differences in weights are not as obvious.

Next, fill two containers with sand. Ask the students which container they think is heavier. Ask how they could find out. Then have a child place the containers on the scale. Discuss what happens. (The scale tips one way.) Ask the students how they know which container is heavier. (The heavier object makes the scale tip in its direction.) Let the students continue to fill two containers at a time, estimate which one is heavier, and use the balance scale to check their guess.

Patterns From the Sea

Patterns

To prepare for this activity, gather a collection of small theme-related objects, such as shells, pebbles, fish crackers, and paper fish. Make several sand-and-sea cards by gluing a 2" x 8" strip of sandpaper across a 5" x 8" piece of blue paper.

Work with a small group of students. Place objects on a sand-and-sea card to make a simple pattern, such as pebble, shell, pebble, shell. Have the students identify the pattern and ask them to extend it by adding more items. Repeat the activity with a different pattern. Then divide the students in pairs, and have each child make a pattern on his or her own card. Have the students ask their partners to guess the pattern.

Sink or Float

Experimentation, Observation

Materials

✓ large tub half full of water
✓ various objects that sink or float (plastic shovel, pail, sunglasses, pebbles, toy boat, rubber worm, sand sifter)
✓ 9" x 12" sheet of white paper
✓ 9" x 12" sheets of light blue paper (1 per student or small group)
✓ pencils
✓ sponge or cloth for cleanup

Draw a wavy line across the center of the white paper. Write *sink* at the bottom of the page and *float* above the line. Reproduce the page on light blue paper, one page per child or small group. Then have the students place various objects in the container of water and observe which ones sink and which ones float. Have the children record their findings by drawing pictures of the objects on their papers.

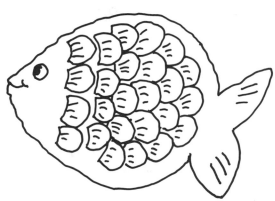

Rainbow Fish

Literature Appreciation, Self-esteem

Materials

✓ *Rainbow Fish* by Marcus Pfister
✓ 3-inch fish-scale shapes cut from metallic wrapping paper or aluminum foil (1 per child)
✓ scissors
✓ marker
✓ large fish outline drawn on mural paper
✓ photo of each student
(You may wish to do this activity after school pictures have been taken.)

Read *Rainbow Fish* to your class. Then do this activity, which focuses on each student's specialness. First, place the photos face down in the center of a circle and give each child a scale. Next, call on a student to pick up a photo and then give away his or her scale to that person. The action must be accompanied by a positive comment about the child receiving the scale. That child responds with a thank you and takes a turn picking a photo from the pile. The game continues until everyone has given away a scale and received a positive comment. Afterwards, let the children glue their scales to the large fish outline for a colorful classroom display.

Down in the Deep Blue Sea

Music

Teach this action song to your class.
The words are sung to the tune of "Shoo Fly."

1. Down in the deep blue sea,
   Down in the deep blue sea,
   Down in the deep blue sea,
   What will we see?

2. We'll see a swimming fish,
   We'll see a swimming fish,
   We'll see a swimming fish,
   That is what we'll see.

3. We'll see an octopus. . .

4. We'll see a great big whale. . .

Have your students make up actions for each verse as
they sing the song. Later, let the children add their own verses to the song.

Extension:
Have the class make stick puppets of the animals. Distribute the puppets
and have each child hold up his or her puppet when the appropriate verse is sung.

A Day at the Beach

Culminating Activity

Having a picnic at a "beach" is the perfect way to end
the Sand and Sea unit! Let children help you make
simple snacks such as peanut butter sandwiches. Cut
bread into fish shapes with cookie cutters or serve
some goldfish crackers. Include some fruit and juice.

Spread out some beach towels either inside the classroom or out on the grass. Pass out the food. Then join
in the fun as your students enjoy their "day at
the beach"!

Sea Animals

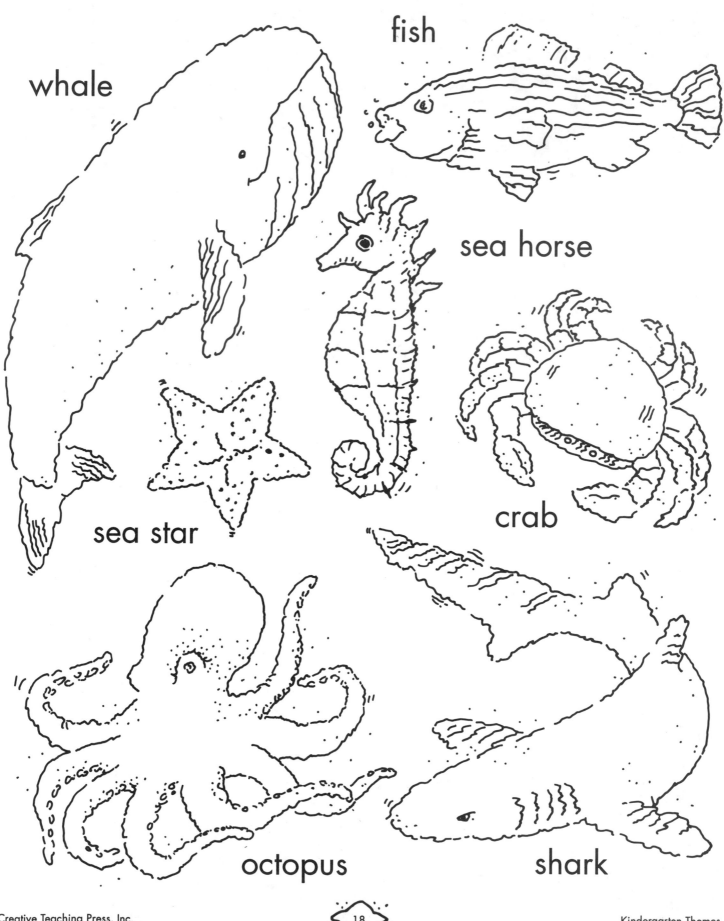

whale

fish

sea horse

sea star

crab

octopus

shark

19

Transportation

Take your students on a fun adventure exploring things that go! This unit includes suggestions for studying different forms of transportation, racing boats, creating vehicles from recycled materials, and other great ideas!

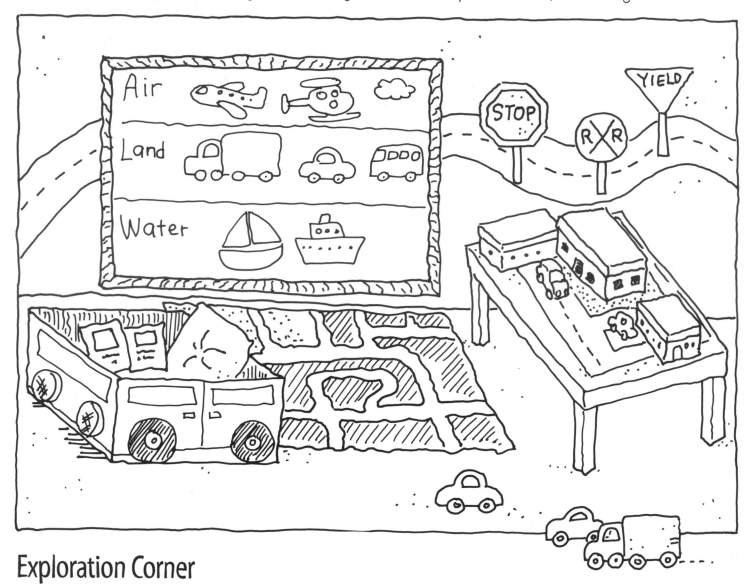

Exploration Corner

Here are some ideas for creating a Transportation Exploration Corner:

➤ Cover a bulletin board with white paper and draw lines to separate it into three horizontal sections. Label the top *Air*, the middle *Land*, and the bottom *Water*. Have the class help you by sponge-painting the sky blue and gluing on cottonball clouds. Let the students cover the land with torn pieces of green paper and color the water with blue crayons or paint. Post pictures of various vehicles in the appropriate sections.

➤ Make colorful cars that children can sit in for reading. For each car, staple tagboard wheels to the sides of a large box. Draw doors and windows or cut some out from paper and glue them on. Add paper headlights. Place a large pillow and several theme-related books inside each car.

➤ Make traffic signs from paper and tape them to the wall.

➤ Cover a table with white butcher paper. Use markers to draw roads on the paper. Cover shoeboxes with paper and turn them into buildings by drawing on doors and windows. Use the lids for roofs. Store crayons, markers, pencils, and scissors inside. Place toy vehicles beside the buildings to complete your "Tabletop Town."

Suggested Activities for the Exploration Corner

Set out activities that allow children to explore the Transportation theme independently. Here are some suggestions:

➤ Store toy vehicles in a container. Invite the class to examine the vehicles and discover how each one moves.

➤ Lay out a vinyl floor mat that displays a town map. (This mat is sold in toy stores.) Let your students move toy vehicles around the map. Or, use wide strips of masking tape to make roads on the floor, and have the students push the vehicles along the various paths.

➤ Make a parking garage from a large shallow box. Cut a wide door on one side of the box. Draw lines inside the box for parking spaces. Have the students take turns "driving" toy vehicles into the garage and parking them in the marked spaces.

➤ Set out rulers and tape measures for measuring the lengths of various vehicles.

➤ Display flyers, calendars, and magazines that show cars, trucks, and other vehicles. (Car dealerships may be able to provide you with colorful brochures.) Have the children look through the materials and pick out the vehicles they would like to own one day.

➤ Provide Legos, Tinkertoys, or other connecting toys for creating vehicles.

➤ Set out activity sheets that feature vehicles (such as dot-to-dot puzzles and mazes).

Books to Share

Here are some colorful books to include in your Transportation study.

Airport by Byron Barton

Airplane, Flying, Freight Train, Harbor, School Bus, and *Trucks* by Donald Crews

Boats, Boats, Boats by Joanna Ruane

Big Wheels by Anne Rockwell

Cars and Trucks and *Things That Go* by Richard Scarry

Hiawatha Passing by Jeff Hagen

The Little Engine That Could by Watty Piper

Round Trip by Ann Jonas

Thomas the Tank Engine Series by W. Awdry

Activities

Land, Air, or Water

Classification

Get 12" x 18" sheets of green, white, and blue paper. You will need one sheet of each color. Print *land* on the green paper, *air* on the white paper, and *water* on the blue paper. Put a collection of toy vehicles in a pillowcase or a bucket. Call on one student at a time to pick up a vehicle, identify it, and state whether the vehicle moves on land, in the air, or on water. Then have the student place the vehicle on the appropriate sheet of paper.

When all the vehicles have been sorted, make a chart with three columns labeled *Land, Air,* and *Water.* Have the students name vehicles for each category while you list them on the chart.

Extension:
Cut out the picture cards on pages 29 and 30. Glue each picture onto a 4-inch tagboard square. Let one or two students at a time play with the cards and sort the pictures according to where each vehicle travels.

Vehicle Show-and-Tell

Oral Language

Set aside a day for Vehicle Show-and-Tell Day. Invite students to bring in a favorite toy vehicle. Let each child display and discuss his or her vehicle, and allow time for the child to answer questions from the class. Display the vehicles on a shelf or a table.

Variation:
Involve parents in your Transportation study by inviting them to bring their vehicles to school for observation. If some parents own or operate special vehicles (such as an ambulance, police car, fire truck, gardening truck, or boat), ask if they would show those to your class. Schedule one parent per day. Encourage parents to share some basic information about their vehicles and tell how they are used. For a special memento, take photos of the students next to their parents and family. Later, have the class use the Transportation multipurpose page (page 31) to write thank-you notes to the parents.

Transportation Through the Years

Social Studies, Art

Ask your students how they would travel to see a friend who lives 100 miles away (by car, train, or plane). Tell them that long ago walking was one of the few ways people could get from one place to another. Explain that over the years many different forms of transportation were invented to make travel easier. Tell the class that for thousands of years people only traveled by land or water; today people can also travel by air. Then show library books that present different kinds of vehicles.

For a follow-up activity, have your students create models of the different forms of transportation used through the years. Here are some suggestions:

Raft – Prehistoric people built rafts from logs or reeds. To make a simple model, have the children glue craft sticks across a 4-inch tagboard square.

Sailing Ship – Early people sailed ships with wide, rectangular sails. Your students can make one by taping a craft stick to the back of a 3" x 4" paper sail. Then give each child a 2" x 5" piece of brown construction paper folded in half lengthwise and stapled at each end. Have each student tape the craft stick inside the paper. To keep the ship standing up, tape it to a 4" x 7" piece of blue construction paper.

Covered Wagon – Have each child bring a shoebox (without a lid) and paint it. When the box is dry, have the children glue a sheet of white paper to the sides of the box to create a canopy. Have them draw spokes on four cardboard wheels and glue the wheels onto the wagons.

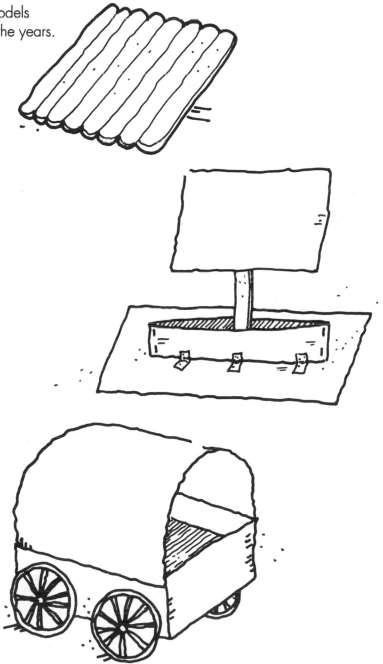

Steam Locomotive – Locomotives move trains on railroad tracks. At one time, all trains were pulled by steam locomotives. Have your students make a model of one. Each child needs a rectangular facial tissue box, a square facial tissue box, a paper cup, and four large cardboard wheels.

Tell the students to turn their boxes upside down and glue the square box onto the rectangular one as shown. Tape the boxes together for extra support. Have the students glue the paper cup near the front of the locomotive as shown. Tape for extra support. Then instruct the children to paint their locomotives. When dry, let the students glue a large paper "window" on each side of the square box. Have them glue two wheels to each side of the locomotive.

Bus – Each student needs a rectangular facial tissue box and four cardboard wheels. Instruct the students to paint the sides and bottoms of their boxes. When dry, tell them to cut out windows and doors from colored paper and glue them onto the boxes. (The bottom of the box will be the top of the bus.) Have each child glue two wheels to each side of the bus.

Plane – Show your students how to fold a 9" x 12" sheet of lightweight paper to make a paper plane. Have your students decorate the plane and tape the ends shut.

Fold paper in half.

Open to reveal fold line.

Fold top corners to center.

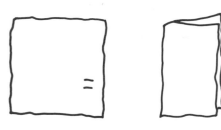

Fold paper in half. Then fold sides down.

Tape the edges shut.

School Bus Safety

Safety Awareness, Fine-Motor Skills

Share *School Bus*, by Donald Crews, with your students. Then arrange for a school bus tour. Invite the bus driver to point out some interesting features of a school bus and explain safety rules to the class. Upon returning to the classroom, provide each student with a sheet of yellow paper, a sheet of black paper, and a bus stencil. Instruct students to trace a bus shape on the yellow paper and cut it out. Then have them cut out a door, several windows, and four wheels from black paper and glue them onto the bus. Have each child dictate a bus safety rule to you as you write it on his or her bus. Display the buses on a bulletin board titled "Safety First."

Safety Chant

Oral Language

Teach your class this delightful chant:

When it's time to go, you have to decide
In what kind of vehicle you will ride.
A car or a truck? A bus or a plane?
A van or a bike? A boat or a train?
Decide what to ride. It's fun, you know.
But learn the safety rules before you go.

Have your students say the chant and clap to the beat. Afterwards, discuss safety rules for bikes, motorcycles, cars, buses, boats, and planes. (Examples: *Ride your bike on the right-hand side of the street. Always wear your seat belt in a car. Wear a life jacket when you ride in a boat.*) Write each safety rule on a strip of paper. Then have each child illustrate a rule. Display the pictures and safety rules in the classroom.

Race Down the Ramp

Measuring Length, Graphing

Make a ramp by taping a sheet of cardboard to a tabletop. The sheet must be long enough to reach the floor. Then have each student choose a toy vehicle. Let one child at a time send his or her vehicle down the ramp. Once a vehicle has stopped moving, use a tape measure or yardstick to measure the distance it traveled from the edge of the ramp. Record the distance on a sheet of chart paper. Afterwards, make a bar graph showing the results.

Extension:
Let the students experiment to find out if they can change the results of the race. For example, have the students change the incline of the ramp by shortening or lengthening the sheet of cardboard used.

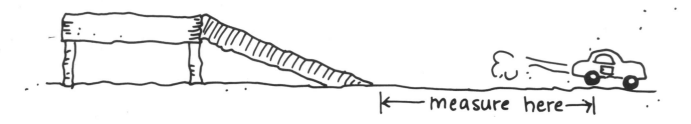

measure here

Boat Race

Prediction, Comparing Time

Place two or more toy boats in a large pan of water. Set an electric fan nearby. (Make sure your students do not attempt to touch the fan once it has been turned on.) Ask the students to predict which boat will move faster when the fan is on. Then turn on the fan and let the wind blow! Have the class observe which boat reaches the other end of the pan first.

Extension:
Use a stopwatch to time one boat at a time as it moves across the water while the fan is turned on. Record the times on chart paper and compare the results. Discuss with students why they think they got the results they did. Ask questions such as the following: *Did the size or shape of the boat make a difference? Did the boats all move in the same way or in different ways?*

What Did You Ride?

Making Comparisons

Reproduce the vehicles on page 29 and cut the cards apart. Glue each picture onto a large sheet of butcher paper that has been divided into six columns. Divide each column into as many sections as you have students. Post the paper at the front of the classroom.

Point to the first picture on the chart and ask the students to raise their hands if they have ever ridden in that vehicle. Have the children help you count the number of hands. Then use a wide highlighting pen to color that many sections on the chart.

Continue the procedure with the other vehicles. Afterwards, have the class look at the chart to see which vehicle has been ridden by the most students and which one has been ridden by the fewest.

car	truck	bus	train	ship	plane

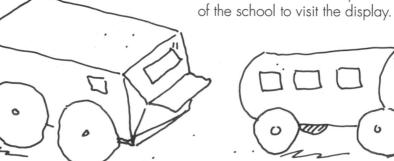

Recycled Vehicles

Art, Recycling Awareness

Discuss with your class the importance of recycling materials. Tell the class that one way children can help recycle is by making new toys from used materials. Then ask your students to bring a variety of scrap materials from home, such as milk cartons, soda bottles, paper cups, bottle caps, foam meat trays, plastic lids, paper tubes, cardboard, yarn, and buttons. Place the materials in a large container. Let the children work in pairs to create unusual vehicles. Show off the vehicles in your room and invite the rest of the school to visit the display.

Transportation Songs

Music

Here are some fun songs your students will enjoy
learning during their Transportation theme study:

"A Bicycle Built for Two"

"Rock-a-Motion Choo Choo" in *We All Live Together,
Volume 1* by Greg and Steve (Youngheart Music/
Creative Teaching Press)

"I've Been Workin' on the Railroad"

"Riding in My Car" and "Yellow Submarine" in *Rockin'
Down the Road* by Greg and Steve (Youngheart
Music/Creative Teaching Press)

"Row, Row, Row Your Boat"

"She'll Be Comin' 'Round the Mountain"

Crunchy Celery Cars

Preparing Food

Let your students make this special snack to celebrate
completion of the Transportation unit:

Materials

✓ piece of celery stalk (1 per student)
✓ cheese spread, cream cheese, or peanut butter
✓ black or green olives
✓ toothpicks (2 per student)
✓ butter knives
✓ small paper plates (1 per student)

Instruct the students to spread cheese or peanut butter
on their piece of celery. Help them insert a toothpick
into each end of the celery. Have the students poke an
olive onto each toothpick for wheels. Invite the students
to eat their snacks while you read a theme-related
storybook.

Transportation Picture Cards

car

truck

bus

train

ship

plane

Transportation Picture Cards

hot-air balloon

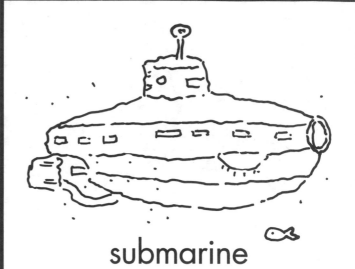

submarine

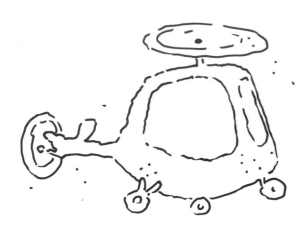

helicopter

sailboat

rowboat

space shuttle

Bugs

Introduce your class to the amazing world of bugs. Your students will go on a bug hunt, examine live specimens, and learn fascinating facts about "creepy-crawlies"!

Exploration Corner

Create a Bugs Exploration Corner that allows children to examine bugs closely. (The term *bugs* in this unit refers to insects—six-legged creatures that have three main body parts—and small creatures such as spiders and centipedes.) Here are some ideas:

❀ Display plastic bugs or stuffed toy insects in a basket.

❀ Arrange theme-related books on a table or shelf. Place small bugs around the books.

❀ Tape a large spiderweb and spiders on the wall. You can buy these items from a party store (especially during the fall) or make them from paper.

❀ Make a border of paper leaves around a bulletin board and arrange pictures of bugs in the middle.

❀ Display a wasp's nest, a honeycomb, or a cocoon if you have one.

❀ Set out magnifying glasses and collections of live bugs. See page 34 for details.

Suggested Activities for the Exploration Corner

Your students will be eager to work with bugs! Here are some activities that will stimulate their interest:

✿ Set out live bugs for students to examine. You can get commercially packaged kits, such as ant farms, or create your own collections. See page 34 for details.

✿ Put out playdough, toothpicks, and small pieces of pipe cleaners. Have the students create their own bugs with the materials.

✿ Fill a large shallow box with soil. Add rocks, twigs, and artificial greenery. Let the students put plastic bugs in the box to create a scene, placing them under or behind rocks, on twigs, and around the greenery.

✿ Store bug stickers and sheets of drawing paper together. Have the children create colorful pictures by drawing tall plants such as grass, weeds, and flowers and then attaching the stickers to their drawings.

Books to Share

Share these intriguing books with your class:

Amazing Anthony Ant by Lorna and Graham Philpot

The Butterfly Alphabet Book by Jerry Pallotta

Butterfly Story by Anca Hariton

Creepy, Crawly Baby Bugs by Sandra Markle

The Grouchy Ladybug, The Very Hungry Caterpillar, The Very Quiet Cricket, and *The Very Busy Spider* by Eric Carle

I Love Spiders by John Parker

In the Garden and *Underfoot* by David Schwartz (Creative Teaching Press)

The Amazing World of Butterflies and Moths by Louis Sabin

The Icky Bug Alphabet Book and *The Icky Bug Counting* Book by Jerry Pallotta

Spiders, Spiders Everywhere and *The Bugs Go Marching* by Rozanne Lanczak Williams (Creative Teaching Press)

How Many Bugs in a Box? by David A. Carter

Miss Spider's Tea Party by David Kirk

Inch by Inch by Leo Lionni

Insect Metamorphosis by Ron and Nancy Goor

Activities

Bug Collections

Observation

Collect some bugs and display them in the Exploration Corner. Let your students use magnifying glasses to examine the creatures. Guide the children's observations by asking questions such as these: *How many legs does the bug have? Does the creature have wings? What color is the bug? How does the animal move? Does it make noise?* When your class is finished examining the bugs, release the creatures outdoors.

Here are some suggestions for setting up bug collections in your classroom.

Caterpillars

Cover the bottom of a large jar with soil. Add a small container of water and stand a leafy twig in it. (Since caterpillars eat only certain kinds of leaves, be sure to choose the same kind of twig as the one on which you found the caterpillar.) Put the caterpillar in the jar. Place a nylon mesh covering on top of the jar and secure it with a rubber band.

Spiders

Put a layer of soil on the bottom of an aquarium tank. Stand up twigs in the dirt (place rocks around the base if necessary) to provide supports for any web that the spider might make. Add a small container of water. Put the spider in the tank. Place a nylon mesh covering on top of the aquarium and secure it with string. (If you are planning to keep the spider for more than several days, you'll need to provide flies for food.)

Ants

Scoop up some soil containing ants and pour the soil in a large jar. Add enough soil to fill half the jar. Add some jam, ripe fruit, and seeds to the jar for food. Cover the top of the jar with a piece of heavy cardboard. Place the jar in a pie plate of water to keep the ants from escaping. Cover the jar with a piece of dark cloth since the ants will feel more comfortable in a dark environment. Remove the cloth when you want to observe the ants. Every so often spray the soil with water to give the ants something to drink.

A Bug Hunt

Observation

Take your class outdoors on a bug hunt. Have your students look under rocks, in the grass, on tree bark, and on the leaves of plants. Collect specimens in jars that have holes punched in the lids. Let the students bring the bugs into the classroom for observation.

Later, have each student choose one bug and draw its picture. Help the children label their pictures and write where the bugs were found. Have each child dictate one observation about the animal while you write the sentence beside the picture. Post the drawings in the classroom. Release the bugs outdoors after the activity is completed.

Alphabet Bugs

Beginning Letter Sounds

Read Jerry Pallotta's *The Icky Bug Alphabet Book* to your class and point out the different varieties of bugs. Have the children notice the great variety in color and shape.

Later, have your students make a class alphabet book of bugs. Get 26 sheets of drawing paper. Print a letter of the alphabet on the top right-hand corner of each sheet. At the bottom of the paper, write the name of a bug beginning with that letter. Then pass out a page to each student, and have the children make an illustration for each picture. (If you have more than 26 children, include more than one page per letter. For example, the letter *b* can include *butterfly* and *bee*.) Punch three holes on the left-hand side of each page, and place the pages in a binder.

The following are some bugs you may want to include in your book: ant, aphid, bee, butterfly, cockroach, cricket, dragonfly, earwig, firefly, flea, grasshopper, hornet, horsefly, Io moth, Japanese beetle, katydid, ladybug, monarch butterfly, no-see-um, orb weaver, praying mantis, queen bee, red admiral butterfly, scorpion, silverfish, spider, tarantula, termite, unicorn beetle, velvet mite, walking stick, wasp, water spider, yellow jacket, yellow plant bug, zebra butterfly.

Sorting Bugs

Classification

Divide the class into small groups, and give each group a copy of the picture cards on page 42. Instruct the students to cut the cards apart. Then have the members of each group sort the pictures into two categories based on whatever criterion they choose. For example, one group might sort the pictures according to bugs with wings and those without; another group might sort the bugs according to those that have six legs and those that do not. Have each group arrange the pictures on a table. Afterwards, have the class look at the different groupings and determine which criterion was used to sort the pictures.

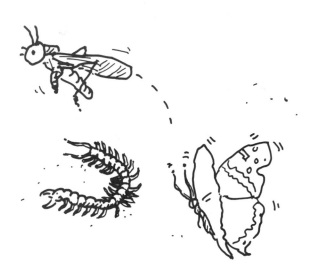

How Bugs Move

Movement, Vocabulary

Hold up pictures of different kinds of bugs and discuss the ways each one moves. Write the corresponding words on the chalkboard or a sheet of chart paper. For example, you might write *crawl, hop, fly, flutter, jump, scurry,* and *inch along.* Then choose one of the bugs. Have your students close their eyes and imagine what it would be like to be that animal. Tell your students to picture where that creature might live. Then have the students open their eyes and move like that animal around the classroom. Repeat the procedure by selecting another bug for the children to imitate.

How Many Bugs in a Box?

Counting

Read David A. Carter's *How Many Bugs in a Box?* to your class. Then do this fun math activity for follow-up. Each day place a different number of plastic bugs in a small box Draw the class's attention to the box by shaking it and saying *I wonder how many bugs are in this box today!* Then during the day, allow one student at a time to open the box, spill out the bugs, and count them. Have each child record the number on a slip of paper and insert the paper into a large envelope that's been labeled *How many bugs?* Have the child keep the number a secret so that other students can count on their own. At the end of the day, open the box and count the bugs with your class. Then open the envelope and see how many correct answers there were.

Bug Problems

Math Word Problems

Prepare some math manipulatives for the class: Make ladybugs by drawing black spots on white beans. Make worms by cutting yarn into pieces 3 inches to 5 inches long. Make caterpillars by stringing 20 buttons onto 5-inch lengths of pipe cleaners and bending the ends of the pipe cleaners inside the button holes.

Have each child cut out a large leaf shape from a 9" x 12" sheet of green paper. Then let the children arrange the "bugs" on their leaves as you recite this math problem: *There were 2 ladybugs on a leaf. Then 1 caterpillar and 1 worm crawled onto the leaf. How many bugs were there on the leaf?* Have the children count their bugs and tell you the answer. Continue the activity with other word problems.

Invite the students to make up their own word problems and record them on a tape recorder. Let the students take turns playing the tape and solving the problems.

Bug Poem

Oral Language, Fine-Motor Skills

Print this poem on chart paper and teach it to your class:

> Big bugs, spotted bugs, bugs with wings,
>
> Bugs with legs and other things,
>
> Bugs that crawl and bugs that fly,
>
> Bugs that jump up very high,
>
> Bugs that wiggle and tickle and crawl,
>
> All kinds of bugs—we love them all!

Have the children recite the poem with you. Then let each child create his or her own unique bug from paper. Post the poem on a bulletin board and arrange the paper bugs around it.

Very Busy Spiders

Retelling a Story

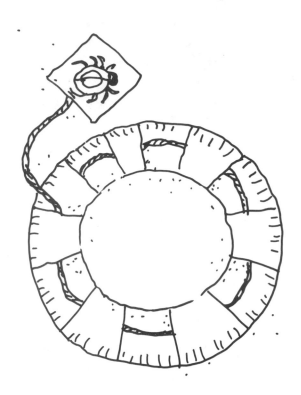

Read Eric Carle's *The Very Busy Spider* to your class. Then have your children make their own webs as they follow along while you retell the story.

Get as many paper plates as you have students. Then cut slits, about one inch apart, around the border of each plate. Give each child a two-inch tagboard square, and tell the student to draw a spider on it. Tape each spider to one end of a four-foot length of yarn. Have each child tape the other end of the yarn to the back of the plate.

As students listen to the story a second time, have each child spin a web by hooking yarn into the notches around the edge of the plate. While they work, have the students chant these sentences: *The spider didn't answer. She was very busy spinning her web.* By the time you finish reading the story, the students will have spun a beautiful web! Let the children take their storytelling webs home to retell the story to their families.

Literature Graph

Literature Appreciation, Graphing

Over the course of a week, read these books by Eric Carle: *The Grouchy Ladybug, The Very Hungry Caterpillar, The Very Quiet Cricket*, and *The Very Busy Spider*. After all the books have been shared, stand them up on the floor. Invite the students to sit behind the book they liked the best. The children will see that the most popular book has the longest line of children while the least popular one will have the shortest line. Take a photo of the class in "graph formation." Write sentence strips telling how many children sat behind each of the books. (For example, you might write *Six students liked <u>The Grouchy Ladybug</u> best.*) Later, when the photo has been developed, display the picture and the sentence strips in the Exploration Corner so that the children can read the sentences to each other.

Hungry Caterpillar Puppets and Song

Days of the Week, Creative Dramatics

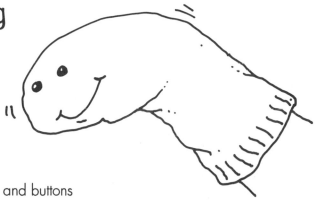

Materials

✓ The *Very Hungry Caterpillar* by Eric Carle

✓ socks (1 per student)

✓ permanent markers or fabric paints

✓ glue

✓ scrap materials, such as sequins, cotton balls, beads, and buttons

Share *The Very Hungry Caterpillar* with students. Discuss the days of the week and the foods that the caterpillar ate each day. Then let each child create a unique caterpillar puppet to review the days of the week. Have each child draw facial features on a sock using markers or fabric paints. Then have the student decorate his or her caterpillar with scrap materials. Let the puppets dry overnight.

Afterwards, have the students hold up their caterpillars and sing the following "Days of the Week Song" to the tune of "Are You Sleeping?"

Sunday, Monday
Tuesday, Wednesday,
Thursday, Friday,
Saturday.

Extension:

Play the song "Days of the Week" from *We All Live Together, Volume 4* by Greg and Steve (Youngheart Music/Creative Teaching Press). Have the caterpillar puppets "sing" the song and tell what they eat each day.

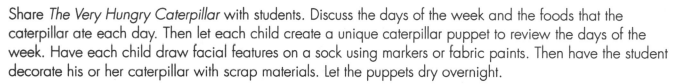

Bug Chants

Rhythm

Reproduce the picture cards on page 42 and cut the cards apart. Provide each student or pair of students with a set of rhythm sticks.

Call on a student to choose a picture and place it in the top of the pocket chart. Then have the students say the bug's name while tapping out the syllables with the rhythm sticks. Have the class chant and tap the word several times. Have another student choose a different picture and repeat the activity.

Extension:

Arrange two picture cards in a line on the pocket chart. Then have the children clap out the name of the first bug and tap their knees to the name of the second. Repeat the pattern several times.

Thumbprint Bugs

Art

Have your students make cute bugs by pressing their thumbs in ink pads and stamping their prints onto paper. Instruct the students to use fine-tipped markers to add features such as legs and antennae. After the children have had a chance to experiment a bit, have them make a border of thumbprint bugs around a sheet of drawing paper. Let the children use their paper to write or draw.

A Parade of Bugs

Patterns

Reproduce several pages of the picture cards on page 42. Cut the cards apart. Then let the students make patterns by arranging the pictures in a row. (For example, one simple pattern is ant, butterfly, ant, butterfly. A more complicated pattern is bee, ladybug, ladybug, grasshopper; bee, ladybug, ladybug, grasshopper). Have the students challenge their classmates to guess the pattern.

Bug Songs

Music

Your students will enjoy learning these fun songs about bugs:

"The Ants Go Marching Down"
"Eentsy, Weentsy Spider"
"Shoo, Fly"
"Spider on the Floor"
"There Was an Old Woman Who Swallowed a Fly"

Tasty Bugs

Food Preparation, Creative Thinking

Materials

- ✓ various food items, such as grapes, peanut butter, cheese spread, crackers, celery, raisins, licorice, and marshmallows
- ✓ toothpicks
- ✓ butter knives
- ✓ paper plates
- ✓ napkins or paper towels

Use the parent letter on page 7 to invite parents to send various food items with their children. Place available foods on paper plates and let the class create some edible bugs. The children can use the following ideas or create their own bugs:

Ants—Spear three grapes with a toothpick.

Ants on a log—Spread peanut butter on celery. Then place raisins on top.

Caterpillars—Poke mini-marshmallows onto a toothpick.

Spiders—Insert 8 short pieces of thin licorice into a marshmallow.

Hold a "Buggy Tea Party" (see the activity below) and let the children eat their tasty bugs at that time.

Buggy Tea Party

Culminating Activity

Read *Miss Spider's Tea Party* and discuss the bugs that attended the party. Then let the students have their own "buggy tea party" and snack on the bugs they made in the "Tasty Bugs" activity described above. Provide some lemonade or apple juice for a refreshing "nectar" to accompany the food.

Bug Picture Cards

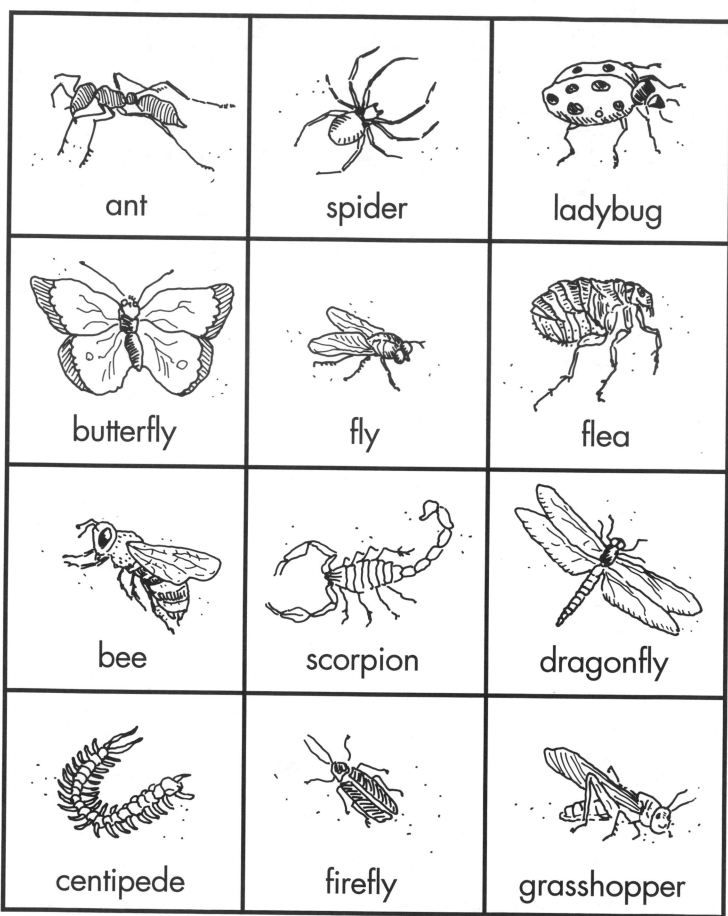

ant	spider	ladybug
butterfly	fly	flea
bee	scorpion	dragonfly
centipede	firefly	grasshopper

Bears

Bears are powerful yet peace-loving animals. Lead your class on a wildlife adventure as they learn about these amazing animals.

Exploration Corner

Create a Bears Exploration Corner that includes a bear's "cave" and other theme-inspired ideas. Here are some suggestions to get you started:

- Spread a blanket or an old sheet over a table to make a "cave." Place a small rug or an old sleeping bag under the table and add some cushions and theme-related books to make a cozy reading area.
- Cut out trees from green butcher paper and tape them to a wall behind the bear's cave to create a forest scene.
- Display pictures of bears on a bulletin board. Include bears from around the world, such as the grizzly bear, the polar bear, the spectacled bear, and the sun bear.
- Arrange teddy bears on a table or a shelf. Invite your students to choose a bear to keep them company whenever they do theme-related activities.
- Keep a container of teddy bear counters handy for students to use during math.

Suggested Activities for the Exploration Corner

Start with the activities below and then add your own creative ideas:

- Cut simple teddy bear shapes from brown paper and store the shapes in a shallow box. Have your students make paper clothes for the bears and glue them on the shapes. Display the bears in the Exploration Corner.

- Provide some stuffed toy bears and a balance scale. Let the children weigh the bears to see which one is the heaviest.

- Set out copies of the Bears multipurpose page (page 55), some teddy bear rubber stamps, several ink pads, and some stencils of bears. Encourage your students to create colorful designs.

- Write these sentences on strips of paper: *I think you are "beary" special! Have a "beary" nice day! I can't bear to be without you!* Let each student make a card by gluing one sentence strip on a sheet of paper that's been folded in half. Have the students decorate their cards and give them to a friend or family member.

Books to Share

Your students will enjoy reading these books about bears.

Alaska's Three Bears by Shelley Gill

Barney Bear Series (Creative Teaching Press)

Bears by Gallimard Jeunesse and Laura Bour

Bears by N. S. Barrett

Corduroy by Don Freeman

Jesse Bear Series by Nancy White Carlstrom

Bear Series by Frank Asch

We're Going on a Bear Hunt by Michael Rosen

Ask Mr. Bear by Marjorie Flack

Winnie-the-Pooh by A. A. Milne

The World of Polar Bears by Virginia Harrison

Activities

Bear Facts

Research, Recall

Read to your class a picture book about bears, such as *Bears* by Gallimard Jeunesse and Laura Bour. Have the children discuss the different facts they learned.

The next day, review the facts with the class. Have the students dictate a fact while you write it on a strip of paper. If the students have forgotten some of the facts, show a page from the book you read to refresh their memory. Afterwards, have each student choose a fact to illustrate. (More than one child may choose the same fact.) Post the sentence strips and the pictures on a bulletin board.

Bears fish for food.

Beary Nice Chart

Critical Thinking

Here's an ongoing activity that will involve your students for the duration of your theme study. First, divide a sheet of chart paper into two columns. Label the first column *What Real Bears Do* and the second column *What Story Bears Do*. Glue a picture of a realistic bear at the top of the first column and a storybook bear, such as Winnie-the-Pooh, at the top of the second column. Post the chart in a convenient location in your classroom.

During your theme study, share a variety of books that present bears as real animals and as storybook characters. As your students learn about bears, have them suggest phrases that describe real and fictional bears. Write the phrases on the chart in the appropriate columns. Continue adding new phrases as your students suggest them.

Is a Bear Like Me?

Attributes, Critical Thinking

Show your class a picture of a bear and a picture of a child. Talk about how the two are different. (Examples: A bear has fur all over its body but a child has comparatively little hair. A bear usually walks on four legs, but a child walks on two.)

After the students have had a chance to think about how bears and people are different, ask them to think about how they are similar. If they have difficulties coming up with ideas, guide them by asking questions such as these: *What kinds of things do you need to live? Who looked after you when you were born?* Then write the following on the chalkboard, adapting the sentences to your students' suggestions:

Is a bear like me? Let's see.

Bears need food. I need food, too.

Bears need water. I need water, too.

Bears need exercise. I need exercise, too.

Bears need sleep. I need sleep, too.

Bears need a family. I need a family, too.

Is a bear like me? Yes, indeed!

Have the students work in pairs or small groups to illustrate the sentences. Combine the drawings into a book for the class to enjoy.

Sharing Bears

Oral Language

Invite the students to share their favorite teddy bears along with fiction and nonfiction books about bears. To make a special "Sharing Chair," cut out a large paper teddy bear and tape it to the back of a chair; let the children sit in the chair when it is their time to share. Display the teddy bears and the books in the Exploration Corner.

All Kinds of Bears

Social Studies

Show your class a globe or a world map. Point out North America, South America, Europe, and Asia. Tell the students that these are the areas where bears live. Then show the class pictures of different kinds of bears. Explain that each bear has its own special characteristics. Tell your students the following facts:

- The **polar bear** lives in the Arctic. It has creamy white fur. It swims better than any other bear.
- The **brown bear** lives in North America, Europe, and Asia. It has brown fur that varies from yellowish to almost black.
- The **black bear** lives in North America and Asia. It is a good tree climber.
- The **sloth bear** lives in India. It has shaggy black fur. It also has a white or yellow chest mark that looks like a *U*, *V*, or *Y*. The sloth bear moves very slowly.
- The **spectacled bear** lives in South America. It has circles of white fur around its eyes, which make it look like it is wearing spectacles (glasses).
- The **sun bear** lives in southeast Asia. It is the smallest bear. It has black fur and a gray or orange nose.

Later, pass out copies of the picture cards found on page 54. Have the class color the bears the appropriate colors. Then tell the students to cut the cards and staple them together to make a booklet.

A Stand-up Bear

Art, Fine-Motor Skills

Make copies of the bear pattern on page 53. Reproduce the page on tagboard. After the students cut out the bear, let them sponge-paint the animal with white, brown, or black paint. Let the pictures dry. Afterwards, have the children cut slits in the feet as indicated. Then give each child a 1" x 12" tagboard strip and instruct the class to put the strips through the slits so that the bears can stand up.

Going on a Bear Hunt

Literature Appreciation

Read Michael Rosen's *We're Going on a Bear Hunt* to the class. In this story, a family goes from one place to another in search of a bear. As they go through grass, swim through water, and so on, delightful sounds are used to describe the actions. Let the children do the following motions as you say the "sounds":

- going through grass—*swishy swashy* (pretend to move the tall grass by making a pushing motion with the left hand and then the right)
- going through water—*splash splosh* (make swimming motions)
- going through mud—*squelch squerch* (lift feet high and take several steps)
- going through a forest—*stumble trip* (clap hands twice and then slap legs)
- going through a snowstorm—*hooooo* (hug self and shiver)
- going through a cave—*tip toe* (tip toe)

Find the Bears

Game, Art

Play this game as a fun follow-up activity to Michael Rosen's *We're Going on a Bear Hunt*.

First, cut teddy bears from 6" x 9" sheets of brown paper—you will need one bear per child. While your students are out for recess or for lunch, hide the bears in the classroom. Also set out art supplies (such as crayons, markers, scissors, and colored paper) on tables around the room.

When the children return to the room, tell them that they are going on a bear hunt. Then have them look around the room for the bears. Tell your students that once they have found a bear, they are to go to one table with art supplies. There, the students complete their bears by adding facial features, clothes, and other items. After all the bears have been found and decorated, display them in the classroom.

Goldilocks and the Three Bears

Creative Dramatics

Familiarize your students with the story "Goldilocks and the Three Bears" by reading it to them. Then let the children present the story on their own.

First, tape-record yourself reading the story. Leave the cassette and tape recorder in a corner of the room. Have four students at a time go to the corner and practice a presentation of the story. The children may either act out the story or put on a puppet show with stick puppets. For the students who plan to act out the story, provide such props as different-sized chairs, bowls, and carpet squares (for the bears' beds). For the students who want to use puppets, provide art supplies for making the puppets and a table covered with an old sheet for the puppet stage. Afterwards, have the groups present their versions of the story to the class.

Bears, Bears, Everywhere!

Oral Language

Teach your class this poem, which has been adapted from *Bears, Bears, Everywhere* (Creative Teaching Press Learn to Read series):

Bears, bears, everywhere!
Bears in squares.
Bears in chairs.
Bears climb stairs.
Bears pay fares.
Bears chase hares.
Bears eat pears.
Bears like fairs.
Bears can scare.
Bears curl hair.
Bears, bears, everywhere.
I love bears!

Say the poem together. Then repeat the poem, but this time have the children clap as they say the last word (or syllable) of each line. Later, have pairs of students illustrate one of the lines on a 12" x 18" sheet of drawing paper.

The Bear Went Over the Mountain

Addition, Subtraction

Cut a large mountain from purple paper and tape it to a wall. Sing or chant the following song with the class:

The bear went over the mountain, the bear went over the mountain,

The bear went over the mountain to see what he could see.

At the end of the song, call on a student to move one stuffed bear from one side of the mountain to the other. With the class, recite the number sentence that corresponds with what happened $(0 + 1 = 1)$. Print the number sentence on the chalkboard. Continue the activity until five or more bears are "over the mountain."

Extension:

Take the bears away by moving them one at a time over the mountain and into a laundry basket or box. Record the corresponding subtraction equations.

Bears in a Cave

Counting

Have the students work in pairs for this activity. Each pair needs a paper bowl, 12 index cards numbered from *1* to *12*, and 12 teddy bear counters. Instruct one student to place the bowl upside down on a table for the bears' cave. Then have the student place some teddy bear counters under the bowl. The student's partner then lifts the bowl, counts the bears in the cave, and places the corresponding number card in front of the cave. The first student checks to see that the card is correct before the partners switch roles. Have the children continue the activity until all 12 cards have been used at least once.

Traveling Backpack

Family Activity

Materials

✓ backpack
✓ stuffed bear
✓ 2 or 3 storybooks about bears
✓ crayons
✓ parent letter (see description below)
✓ notebook
✓ marker or pen
✓ clear contact paper

Make one copy of the Bears multipurpose page (page 55). Then write on it the following letter to parents:

> *Dear Parents,*
>
> *In this backpack you will find some books about bears, a stuffed bear, crayons, and a notebook. Please read one or more of the books with your child. Then read the activities listed below and help your child do one of them:*
>
> • *Count the number of teddy bears in your home. Write the number in the notebook. Draw a picture of your favorite bear.*
>
> • *Write one fact about bears and illustrate it.*
>
> • *Choose one of the books you read. Draw a picture of your favorite part.*
>
> *Please return the backpack with its contents to school within two days so other families may enjoy it, too. Thank you!*

Cover the letter with clear contact paper and then place it in the backpack. Add the stuffed bear and the rest of the materials. Send the backpack home with a different child every few days. When students return the backpack to class, have them describe the activities they did.

Bear Pattern

Bear Picture Cards

polar bear

sloth bear

brown bear

spectacled bear

black bear

sun bear

55

Shapes

Shapes are all around us! As you help students identify and examine different kinds of shapes, encourage them to look for shapes in their environment.

Exploration Corner

Here are some ideas for setting up a Shapes Exploration Corner in your classroom.

◆ Decorate a bulletin board with a border of shapes. Post shapes in the middle of the board.

◆ Tape string to the back of large tagboard shapes and hang them from the ceiling.

◆ Collect items that have distinct shapes, such as a clock, a pennant, and a picture frame. Set the items on a table and label each shape.

◆ Post pictures of interesting shapes. For example, display a tire ad that shows a variety of tires arranged across a page.

◆ Cover a table with white butcher paper or a white paper tablecloth. Draw colorful shapes along the edges of the paper.

◆ Display theme-related books on a table. Add art supplies such as crayons, markers, pencils, and papers. Include activity sheets, such as hidden pictures and dot-to-dot puzzles, that focus on shapes.

Suggested Activities for the Exploration Corner

Provide a variety of activities that allow children to explore shapes on their own. Here are some ideas to get you started:

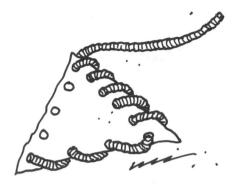

◆ Cut six large tagboard shapes—circle, square, triangle, rectangle, diamond, oval. Write the name of each shape on a card. Punch holes around the edges and tie a string to each shape. Wrap tape around the end of the string to form a "needle." Let the students "sew" by inserting the string through the holes.

◆ Set out attribute blocks and drawing paper. Have the students build pictures by placing the shapes on the paper. Then let the children make a record of each shape by tracing each block onto the paper and coloring the shapes.

◆ Provide colorful paper shapes of different sizes. Have the children glue the shapes onto white paper to make interesting pictures.

◆ Store stencils or patterns of shapes in a tray. Let your students use them to trace shapes onto wrapping paper, construction paper, and tissue paper. Instruct the children to make a shape collage by cutting out the shapes and gluing them onto background paper.

Books to Share

The following shape books are ideal for young students.

Animal Shapes by Brian Wildsmith

Circles, Triangles, Squares and *Shapes, Shapes, Shapes* by Tana Hoban

Color Farm and *Color Zoo* by Lois Ehlert

I See Shapes by Marcia Fries (Creative Teaching Press)

Museum Shapes by Gisela Voss

Pancakes, Crackers, and Pizza: A Book of Shapes by Marjorie Eberts and Margaret Gisler

Shapes by John Reiss

Activities

Shape Scrapbook

Shape Recognition

Make a Shape Scrapbook by stapling six sheets of white paper and two covers together. You will need one booklet for each child. Give each child a copy of the shapes shown on page 66. Instruct the students to cut the cards apart. Tell the children to glue one shape to the top right-hand corner of each page in their scrapbook. Have the students cut out magazine pictures of shapes and glue them onto the appropriate pages. Then have the students decorate the front covers.

Variation:

Make a Shape Scrapbook for each kind of shape. For example, cut circular shaped pages for a book about circles; cut triangular pages for a book about triangles. Have the students glue or draw an appropriate picture for each page.

Shape Search

Shape Recognition

Get several slips of paper and draw a shape on each one. Fold the papers and place them in a shoebox or another container. Let the students take turns choosing a slip of paper from the box, unfolding it, and naming the shape. When a student has named the shape, have him or her look around the classroom for one or more objects of the same shape.

Extension:

Play the song "Round in a Circle" from *We All Live Together, Volume 1* (Youngheart Music/Creative Teaching Press) by Greg and Steve. This lively song will have everyone dancing to the beat as they search for shapes.

Shapes in Nature

Observation

Help each student make a pair of binoculars by stapling two toilet paper tubes together and punching holes near the top. Have the child run string or yarn through the holes and tie the ends together to form a strap. With binoculars and small plastic bags in hand, take your class outside to look for shapes. Tell the students to collect interesting objects, such as rocks and leaves, and store them in their bags. (Remind the class to collect items that, if removed, will not alter the environment significantly. Students should not remove nests or insects, nor should they break off tree branches.) As the children collect their items, have them notice the shape of each. Upon returning to the classroom, have the students glue their collections onto copies of the Shapes multipurpose page (page 67). Help each student write the name of the object and its shape on his or her paper. Gather the collections and display them on a bulletin board titled *Shapes in Nature*.

Shapes Around the School

Observation

Lead your class on a walk through the school. Take photographs of students standing near objects of various geometric shapes. Mount the pictures on poster board and write a caption for each picture. Children will enjoy viewing the pictures and pointing out the various shapes. If a camera is not available or practical, students may draw what they have seen and dictate one or more sentences about their pictures to you.

Sandbox Shapes

Fine-Motor Skills

Call on one pair of students at a time to do this activity. First set out the picture cards of shapes (page 66) and a tub of wet sand. Have the children lay the picture cards face down. One child then picks a picture card and draws the corresponding shape in the sand; his or her partner names the shape drawn and copies it in the sand. The children then switch roles.

Sorting Shapes

Classification

Ask parents for help in collecting interesting items for the class to sort. First write the following letter on the Shapes multipurpose page (page 67).

Dear Parents,

We are collecting objects for our Shapes unit. Can you help? If so, please place two or more small objects of various geometric shapes in the bag. (Buttons, toys, beads, uncooked pasta, and plastic lids are some items that will help us greatly.) The objects will be used for an activity at school. Thank you!

Reproduce one copy of the letter for each student. Then place the letters in resealable plastic bags and send them home with the children. Later, let the students share the objects they have brought to school. Place the donated items in a large gift bag. Also place sorting trays, such as egg cartons, pie plates, and muffin pans, inside the bag. Leave the materials at the Exploration Corner so students can work with them independently. Instruct the children to sort the materials according to shape.

Guess a Shape

Critical Thinking

Materials
- ✓ cloth bag or pillowcase
- ✓ blindfold or piece of soft fabric
- ✓ common household objects of various shapes, such as small picture frames, cookie cutters, and plastic containers

Place the objects in a cloth bag or pillowcase. Blindfold a student and have him or her choose an object from the bag. Challenge the student to feel the object, identify it, and name its shape. Repeat the activity with several other students. Later, leave the items at the Exploration Corner and let the children play the game on their own.

Shape Patterns

Patterns

Divide the class into small groups. Give each group a 4" x 36" piece of colored butcher paper and three copies of the shapes shown on page 66. Instruct the students to cut out the shapes. Then have each group make a pattern by gluing the shapes onto the colored paper. Let the groups show their patterns and describe them to the class.

Variation:

Provide the class with colorful, gummed paper shapes. (These are available in stores that sell art supplies or educational materials.) Have each student attach the shapes to strips of white paper to make a colorful pattern.

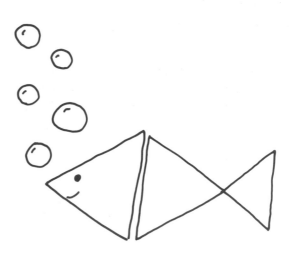

Shapely Pictures

Critical Thinking, Art

Materials
- ✓ paper shapes in many sizes and colors
- ✓ resealable plastic bags
- ✓ 12" x 18" construction paper (1 for each student)
- ✓ glue
- ✓ markers

Divide the class into small groups. Give each group a 12" x 18" sheet of construction paper along with a resealable plastic bag filled with a variety of paper shapes. Challenge the students to create beautiful pictures or designs using the shapes in their bags. Suggest that they arrange the shapes first. When the members of a group decide they all like the design, they can glue the shapes onto their paper. Let the students use markers to add details to their pictures.

After all the groups have completed their pictures, have each group share its work with the class. Have the class point out interesting observations about the shapes used, such as the following: *The group used blue circles to make bubbles and red triangles to make a fish.*

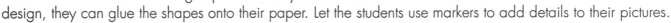

Body Shapes

Problem Solving

Reproduce page 66 and cut the cards apart. Hold up a shape and discuss its attributes with your class. Then call on several students to form the shape with their bodies. For example, if you held up a circle, the children could stand in a circle holding hands. A triangle, on the other hand, could be created by three students, with each child sitting on the floor with legs together and extending straight out to touch the back of the child in front of him or her. Children will enjoy watching their classmates form the various shapes! Repeat this activity several times using different shapes and different sets of students.

A Tangram Story

Literature Appreciation, Critical Thinking

Read Ann Tompert's *Grandfather Tang's Story*. This engaging story uses tangram shapes to illustrate the Chinese tale of two fox fairies. A tangram is a Chinese puzzle made up of seven shapes. The shapes are combined in different ways to create pictures of animals and objects.

After you read the story, go back to some of the pictures and discuss with your class how the different shapes are arranged. Then set out attribute blocks and let your students use them to create interesting animals of their own.

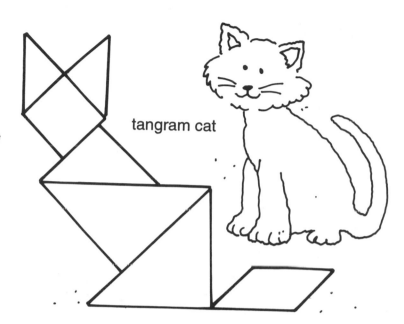
tangram cat

Touchable Shape Posters

Shape Recognition, Tactile Skills

Materials
✓ poster board
✓ various textured materials, such as sandpaper, corduroy, cotton, netting, corrugated cardboard, and bubble wrap
✓ glue
✓ scissors

Cut shapes from the textured materials. Glue each shape to a piece of poster board. Then play this guessing game with small groups of students. Have the students close their eyes. Pass around one of the shapes and let each child take a turn feeling it. Ask the children to identify the shape. When all the students in the group have made a guess, let them open their eyes to check their guess. Repeat the procedure until all the shapes have been felt.

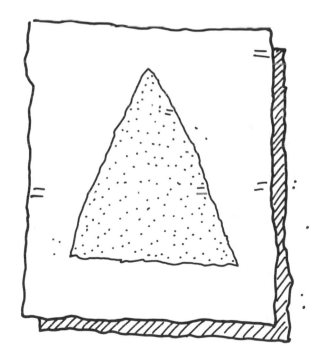

Shape Prints

Art

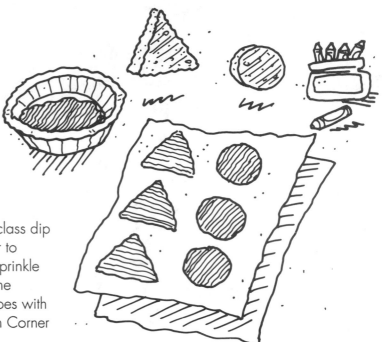

Materials
- ✓ stiff sponges (the type used for cleaning kitchens)
- ✓ paint
- ✓ pie pans or other shallow containers for paint
- ✓ drawing paper
- ✓ glitter (optional)
- ✓ scissors
- ✓ crayons or markers

Cut several shapes from the dry sponges. Have your class dip the sponges in paint and stamp shapes on their paper to create interesting designs. If you like, let the students sprinkle the pictures with glitter before the paint dries. When the pictures are dry, invite the children to outline their shapes with markers or crayons. Post the pictures in the Exploration Corner for a colorful display.

Playground Shapes

Following Directions, Large-Motor Skills

Take your class out to the playground for this lively game. First draw very large shapes with chalk on a paved area. Then let the students run around the playground, staying away from the shapes. When you call out "Shape," all the students must run inside a shape as quickly as they can. Play this game a few more times, and then let the children take turns being the caller.

Variations:
- ◆ Play some music on a tape recorder. When you stop the music, the children must run inside a shape.
- ◆ Draw several large circles, triangles, rectangles, and other shapes. Let the students run around the playground. Then call out the name of a shape. The children must find the corresponding shape. They can either stand completely inside the shape or place only a hand or foot in it.

A Shapes Party

Culminating Activity

Host a Shapes Party to celebrate the completion of this theme study. Let the children help you prepare the following foods for the party.

Biscuit Shapes

Cooking, Fine-Motor Skills

Get 3 tubes of refrigerated biscuits. Give a piece of biscuit dough to each child and have the students form them into various shapes. Place the shapes on a cookie sheet, and bake according to directions. Let cool. If you like, let the students add a topping (such as peanut butter, jam, or margarine) to their biscuits before eating.

Variation:
Make cookie shapes using rolls of prepared cookie dough.

A Bag of Shapes

Measurement

Set out bowls of small foods that come in circles and squares, such as Cheerios, Fruit Loops, Corn Chex, and Quaker Life. Then post a sheet of paper with this recipe: *Add 3 tablespoons of circles and 3 tablespoons of squares to a bag. Mix and enjoy!* Give each child a resealable plastic bag and a tablespoon. Have the students follow the recipe to fill their bags with a tasty assortment of edible circles and squares.

Shape Sandwiches

Food Preparation, Fine-Motor Skills

Let your class use cookie cutters to cut shapes from bread. Have the students spread a topping (cream cheese, grated cheese, peanut butter, or other foods) on each shape to make a delicious sandwich.

Shape Picture Cards

circle

square

rectangle

triangle

diamond

oval

Colors

Color adds beauty and interest to our world. Help your students discover and experiment with colors as they make color collages, mix colored water, look for rainbows, and more!

Exploration Corner

Create an exciting Colors Exploration Corner in your classroom. Add your own colorful ideas to these suggestions.

- Draw a large rainbow on butcher paper. Let your students help you color it with markers or cover it with pieces of tissue paper. Tape the rainbow to the wall. Add puffy clouds made from cotton batting.
- Make a colorful garden by taping large paper flowers along the wall.
- Display colorful paper butterflies.
- Hang balloons or tissue paper streamers near a window.
- Set out easels with paper, paints, and paintbrushes.
- Cover a table with a brightly colored tablecloth. Display theme-related books on the table.

Suggested Activities for the Exploration Corner

Here are some fun, challenging activities that allow children to explore colors independently.

- Set out small sheets of blue, yellow, and red cellophane paper. Have the students overlap two colors at a time to see new colors appear.
- Provide crayons, markers, chalk, and colored pencils. Include various shades of each color. Let the students draw with different mediums to see the kinds of colors that are produced.
- Fill some baby food jars with colored water. (Color the water with red, blue, and yellow food coloring.) Set the jars on a table. Have the students place one jar in front of another to see the colors "mix."
- Put out containers of small items, such as plastic eggs, fabric scraps, buttons, toys, and attribute blocks. Have the students sort the items by color and arrange them on paper plates.

Books to Share

Here are some books about color to include in your theme study.

Brown Bear, Brown Bear, What Do You See? by Bill Martin Jr.

The Crayola Counting Book by Rozanne Lanczak Williams (Creative Teaching Press)

Harold and the Purple Crayon by Crockett Johnson

I See Colors by Rozanne Lanczak Williams (Creative Teaching Press)

Is It Red? Is It Yellow? Is it Blue? and *Of Colors and Things* by Tana Hoban

Little Blue and Little Yellow by Leo Lionni

The M&M's Counting Book by Barbara Barbieri-McGrath

Mouse Paint by Ellen Stoll Walsh

My Crayons Talk by Patricia Hubbard

Red, Green, Blue, and Yellow by Gabrielle Woolfitt

Seven Blind Mice by Ed Young

Activities

Color Days

Color Recognition

Celebrate different "Color Days" during your theme study. For each Color Day, focus on a particular color by implementing one or more of the following activities:

- Have your class wear clothing that matches the color of the day.
- Ask the students to bring appropriately colored objects from home and share them with the class.
- Let the children complete activity sheets using the color of the day. For example, on "Green Day," children can complete phonic worksheets or dot-to-dot puzzles with green crayons or markers.
- Have the class make a "Color Collage" as described below.

Color Collage

Color Recognition, Art

Have the students work together to make an interesting collage for each color. First, ask the students to bring from home disposable objects of a particular color. Tell the class that the objects must be small and light enough so that they can be attached to a poster. Items may include buttons, paper or fabric scraps, pipe cleaners, plastic lids, ribbons, yarn, and beads.

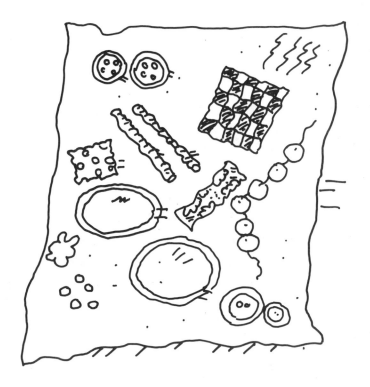

When the children bring the objects to school, have them glue or tape them on a large sheet of butcher paper to make a colorful collage. Write the name of the color on the paper. Then display the collage on a bulletin board or wall.

Color Booklets

Color Recognition, Matching

Make Color Booklets by stapling together eight sheets of white paper and two construction paper covers. You will need one booklet for each child.

Give each child a copy of the picture cards on page 78, and have the students color the pictures as marked. Then instruct the students to cut the cards apart. Tell the children to glue one card to the top right-hand corner of each page in their booklet. Have the students cut out magazine pictures, fabric scraps, wrapping paper, and other flat materials of specific colors and glue them on the corresponding pages. Have the students complete the booklets by decorating the front covers.

Colors in Nature

Color Recognition, Observation

Invite your students to bring objects from nature that show off specific colors. For example, the children might share leaves, flowers, rocks, feathers, shells, and coral. Have the students help you sort the objects by color, and then arrange them on a table. Complete the display with pictures of animals (such as butterflies and parrots) and other things from nature that are made up of interesting colors.

Beautiful Butterflies

Art

Show pictures of butterflies to your class. Discuss the bright colors of some of these creatures. Then have your students make beautiful butterflies of their own.

Give each student a sheet of white paper and instruct the class to fold the papers in half. Have the children unfold their papers and use eyedroppers to squeeze drops of paints onto the fold line. Then have them refold the papers and press down to make the paint spread. Let the students open their papers to see the beautiful designs inside. When the paint has dried, help the children cut the papers into butterfly shapes.

Color Word Match

Recognizing Color Words

Get eight colors of construction paper. Cut a 4-inch square from each paper, and place the squares in a pocket chart. Next, write the color words on index cards using markers of corresponding colors. (For example, write *red* with a red marker.) Have the students take turns placing each color word beside the paper of the corresponding color.

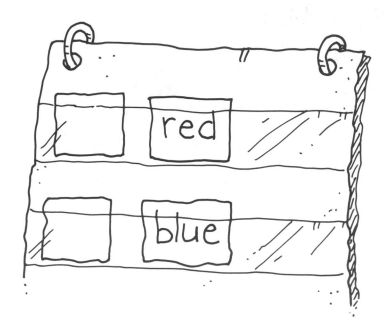

Color Poems

Creative Writing

Read your students portions of Mary O'Neill's *Hailstones and Halibut Bones*. This classic book features a poem for each color. The title of a poem always begins with "What Is . . .?" In the poems, O'Neill discusses how the various senses are stirred by a particular color.

After sharing the book with your students, have them write a class poem for a color. Begin by choosing a color and brainstorming descriptive phrases that might work in the poem. Write the students' ideas on the chalkboard. Then have the children choose which phrases could be used to construct the poem. Write the poem on chart paper and display it on a bulletin board. Have the students draw pictures to accompany the poem.

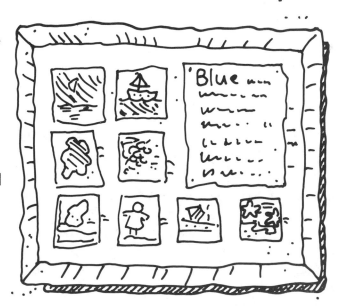

Extension

Play the song "What Is Pink?" from *Kids in Motion* by Greg and Steve (Youngheart Music/Creative Teaching Press). Have the students listen carefully and draw each item that is mentioned in the song.

Mixing Paints

Literature Appreciation, Experimentation

Share Ellen Stoll Walsh's *Mouse Paint* with your class. Talk about the new colors that were made when the mice mixed combinations of blue, red, and yellow. Then provide the class with paints, brushes, and paper. Set out pie plates or foam trays for mixing two colors together. Have the students mix the paints to see if they get the same results as the mice.

Extension:

Ask the class to help you make a chart that shows the secondary colors created when pairs of primary colors are mixed.

Color Graphs

Graphing

Reproduce the color cards on page 78. Color the pictures the appropriate colors, and then cut the cards apart. Glue the cards vertically on a large sheet of butcher paper so that the cards are directly beneath one another.

Give each child a 2" paper circle, and have the students write their names on the circles. Then let the students tape their circles beside the color they like best. Afterwards, have the students count the number of circles for each color to decide which color is the most popular in their class.

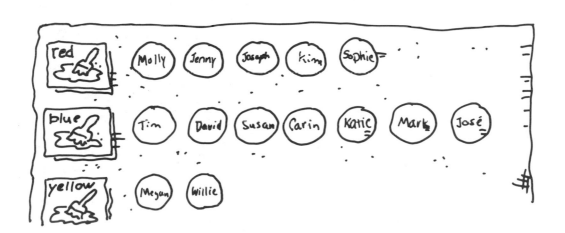

Color Filter Frames

Experimentation

Materials

- ✓ several sheets of cardboard
- ✓ colored cellophane of different colors
- ✓ scissors
- ✓ masking tape

Cut several cardboard frames and tape colored cellophane to each one. Invite the students to look through the frames. Ask them to describe how the paper affects what they see. Then have the students lay one frame over another in order to combine two colors. Ask the children to describe what happens to the colors.

Tissue-Paper Bottles

Mixing Colors, Art

Materials

- ✓ glass bottle with a narrow neck, such as a salad dressing bottle (1 for each child)
- ✓ small pieces of tissue paper
- ✓ pie plates or foam trays (for holding the tissue paper)
- ✓ container of liquid starch
- ✓ paintbrushes
- ✓ newspaper
- ✓ clear finish (optional)

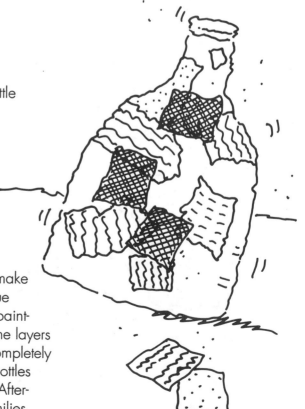

Cover the work surface with newspaper. Then have the children make colorful vases by covering their bottles with different colors of tissue paper. Have the children attach the paper by dabbing at it with paintbrushes dipped in liquid starch. Talk about what happens when the layers of tissue paper overlap. (The colors mix.) When the bottles are completely covered, set them aside overnight. When dry, you can take the bottles outdoors and spray them with a clear finish for a beautiful shine. Afterwards, let the students take their vases home as a gift for their families.

See a Rainbow

Experimentation

Materials

✓ books about rainbows, including *Skyfire* by Frank Asch and *Rain* by Donald Crews
✓ table
✓ prisms
✓ sunny window

Share stories about rainbows with your students. Explain that rainbows appear when sunlight shines through tiny drops of water and is split into different colors. Then let your students make their own rainbows on a sunny day. First, place a table near a sunny window. Then have the children experiment by holding a prism near the window. (Do this activity early in the day or in the late afternoon when the sun's rays are more slanted.) If a student holds the prism at just the right angle, he or she will be able to see a rainbow on the table. Explain that when sunlight passes through the prism, it is split into different colors—just as it is split when it shines through drops of water in the air.

Raindrop Designs

Mixing Colors, Art

Materials

✓ 3 or more jars of water
✓ red, yellow, and blue food coloring
✓ eyedroppers (1 per student)
✓ coffee filters (3–4 per student)
✓ newspaper

Cover the work surface with newspaper. Color the water with food coloring. Then let small groups of children take turns using eyedroppers to squeeze drops of water onto their coffee filters. Show the children how they can mix the colors by dropping one color on top of another. Let the children make 3 or 4 coffee filter designs. When the filters have dried, hang them in the Exploration Corner for a colorful display.

Color Race

Large-Motor Skills, Listening Skills

Materials

✓ small objects of various colors
✓ laundry basket
✓ red, blue, yellow, green, orange, purple, black, brown construction paper (1 sheet per color)

Divide the class into two teams and have them sit in two lines. Place the objects in the laundry basket and set the basket several feet away from the students. Place the colored sheets of paper in a row on the floor.

Call out a color. As soon as the color is called, one child on each team runs to the basket to find something of that color. Each child picks up the object and places it on the corresponding sheet of paper. Repeat the activity with another pair of students. Continue the race until all the students have had a chance to run.

Color Run

Large-Motor Skills, Listening Skills

Here's a fun game that can be played either indoors or outdoors. To begin, have the children spread out and run freely. Without warning, call out a color. As soon as the children hear the color, they must run and touch something of the corresponding color. (Tell the children that they are not allowed to touch their classmates' clothing; they are to only touch items that are part of the environment.) As soon as everyone is touching an item, let the children run again before you call another color. Repeat the activity several times.

Rainbow Bananas

Food Preparation, Color Recognition

Materials
- ✓ bananas
- ✓ knife (for teacher's use)
- ✓ serving bowls or plates
- ✓ several colors of gelatin
- ✓ paper plates (1 per student)
- ✓ toothpicks
- ✓ margarine tubs or similar containers

Peel and slice several bananas. Place the slices in a bowl or on a plate. Pour a different color of gelatin powder in each container. Let small groups of children take turns picking up the bananas with toothpicks and rolling the slices in the dry gelatin powder. Have each child place his or her colored banana slices on a paper plate. Before the children eat their bananas, have them solve riddles like this: *Think of a color that you see in apples, raspberries, and watermelons. Eat the banana that is that color.*

Rainbow Toast

Food Preparation

Materials
- ✓ milk
- ✓ measuring cup
- ✓ food coloring (4 different colors)
- ✓ new paintbrushes
- ✓ 4 clear plastic cups
- ✓ toaster oven or toaster
- ✓ bread (1 slice for each student)
- ✓ butter
- ✓ butter knives
- ✓ paper plates

Pour $\frac{1}{4}$ cup of milk into each plastic cup. Add a drop of food coloring to each cup and mix so that you have four colors of milk. Have the children paint a rainbow or other colorful design on their bread. Toast the bread and let the children watch the colors brighten up! When done, let the students spread butter on their bread and enjoy their colorful snack.

Color Picture Cards

red

purple

blue

green

yellow

brown

orange

black

Farm Animals

Create "Old MacDonald's Farm" in your classroom and introduce your students to the world of farm animals.

Exploration Corner

Here are some fun ideas for creating an exciting Farm Animals Exploration Corner.

- Draw a large barn from red butcher paper. Tape the barn to a wall.
- Stand a table in front of the barn. Arrange plastic farm animals on the table.
- Stuff potato sacks or feed bags with newspaper and toss them in the corner along with a bale of hay.
- Tape a paper scarecrow to the wall. Cut crows from black paper and arrange them around the scarecrow.
- Stand a wheelbarrow in the corner and display theme-related books in it.

Suggested Activities for the Exploration Corner

Here are some stimulating activities that allow your students to explore the Farm Animals theme on their own.

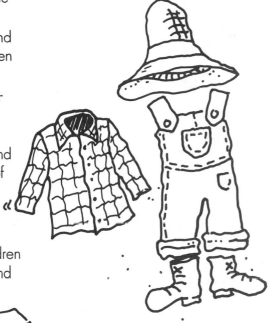

- Set out containers of Legos, wooden blocks, plastic farm animals, and toy vehicles. Cover the bottom of a shallow box with a piece of green carpeting. Let your students build a farm scene in the box.

- Fill a box with clothing such as a farmer might wear: overalls, checkered shirts, wide-brimmed hats, neckerchiefs, work shoes. Invite the students to take turns dressing up as farmers.

- Provide copies of the Farm Animals multipurpose page (page 91) and rubber stamps of farm animals. Have the children stamp a parade of animals across a page.

- Make picture cards by attaching stickers of farm animals to index cards. Let the students use the cards for playing Concentration.

- Place a variety of theme-related activities on a shelf or table for children to do independently—jigsaw puzzles, stencils, dot-to-dot puzzles, and so on.

Books to Share

Your class will enjoy reading these books about the farm.

Barnyard Banter by Denise Fleming

Big Red Barn by Margaret Wise Brown

Color Farm by Lois Ehlert

Inside a Barn in the Country by Alyssa Satin Capucilli

Jane Yolen's Old MacDonald Songbook edited by Jane Yolen

Lucky Russell by Brad Sneed

My Barn by Craig Brown

Over On the Farm by Christopher Gunson

The Very Busy Spider by Eric Carle

Winter on the Farm by Laura Ingalls Wilder

Activities

Farm Mural

Vocabulary Development, Fine-Motor Skills

Kick off your theme study by playing the songs "Heavenly Music" from Greg and Steve's *Playing Favorites* album (Youngheart Music/Creative Teaching Press) and "Down on the Farm" from Greg and Steve's *We All Live Together, Volume 5* (Youngheart Music/Creative Teaching Press). After your students listen to the songs, have them discuss the various types of animals that live on a farm. Display pictures of the animals for the children to study. Then have your class make a colorful farm mural for the classroom. First, have the students paint a simple background scene on a large sheet of butcher paper. Instruct them to paint the top of the paper blue and the bottom brown. When the paint has dried, add a red barn. Next, brainstorm with the class a list of farm animals, and record your students' responses on chart paper. Then have small groups of children take turns painting farm animals on the butcher paper. After the pictures have dried, help your students label the animals on the mural.

Farm Animal Research

Research, Critical Thinking

Tell the students that they will be researching a farm animal. Then give each child a copy of the barn pattern (page 89). Have each child choose a farm animal and draw a picture of it. Then let the students look at library books and glean information about farm animals from the pictures. For example, a picture of a farmer milking a cow shows that cows provide milk; a picture of a horse eating hay gives information about what horses eat. Later, have the students dictate one or more factual statements about their animals while you write the sentences beside the pictures. Let the students share their pictures and facts with the class. If you like, bind the pages into a book for your classroom library.

A hen lays eggs.

Class Field Trip

Observation

Arrange a field trip to a nearby farm. Your class will enjoy observing the various animals and asking questions about what it takes to run a farm. Take photographs of the farm, including pictures of the animals, the farmer, and the different kinds of farm machinery.

After the field trip, have the students review what they saw on the farm. Write their responses on chart paper to make a class report about the field trip. Then have the students draw pictures to show what they enjoyed best about the trip.

Extension:

A field trip offers a great opportunity for students to write thank-you notes. Have the students compose one together, and then write their sentences on a sheet of paper. Have each child sign his or her name at the bottom of the note.

Name That Animal

Word Attack Skills

Write the names of farm animals on index cards; you will need to write one letter per card. Choose one animal name and arrange its letters face down in a pocket chart.

Divide the class into two teams. Have the teams take turns calling out a letter. If a team calls out a letter that is in the animal's name, turn that card over so that the letter is visible. Students may guess the name of the animal as the letters are revealed. Keep playing until all the letters are facing up or until the animal has been correctly identified. Repeat the activity with another animal's name.

Sorting Animals

Classification

Gather a variety of plastic or stuffed farm animals. If toys aren't available, you may use pictures instead.

Place two hula hoops on the floor. Then sort the animals into two groups and place them in the hoops. For example, you could place four-legged animals in one hoop and two-legged animals in the other. Ask the class to look at the groups and tell how the animals were sorted. Repeat the activity, forming two different groups with the animals. (Examples: brown/not brown; small/large) Later, invite one child at a time to sort the animals while the rest of the class guesses what criterion was used.

Barnyard Math

Addition, Subtraction

Get several index cards and write on each one an addition or a subtraction problem (such as $1 + 1 =$ or $2 - 1 =$). Lay the cards on a table along with a collection of plastic farm animals. Call on a group of children to work with you. Give each child in the group a pencil and a copy of the Farm Animals multipurpose page (page 91). Then tell the students a story problem based on one of the problems on the index card. For example you could state the following: *There was 1 cow by the barn. Then 1 horse came to visit her. How many animals were by the barn?* Ask a student to manipulate the farm animals to show the answer. Have the children record the problem and answer on their Farm Animals page. Continue the activity with other problems.

Extension:

Let each student make up a problem and write it on an index card. Have the students exchange their problems with a partner and use the farm animals to find the answers.

Products From Farm Animals

Science

Bring to class some of the following items: butter, empty ice cream carton, milk carton, egg carton, packaged ham, package of frozen chicken dinner, a pillow or sleeping bag stuffed with goose down, and wool material or yarn. Spread the items out on a table.

Tell the students that people rely on farm animals for many products. Then have the class examine the items on the table. Point to each item and discuss the farm animal the product comes from. Repeat the activity with each of the items on the table. Make a chart listing the products and the animals they come from.

Extension:
Have the children look through grocery store flyers and circle the products that come from farm animals.

Farm Animal Charades

Creative Dramatics

Reproduce the farm animals picture on page 90. Glue each one to a piece of construction paper, and lay the pictures face down in a box. Then play Farm Animal Charades. Call on a child to pick up one of the papers and look at the picture. Then have the child pantomime the animal selected. The student who correctly guesses the animal chooses the next picture. Continue the activity, calling on different students to act out the various animals.

Farm Animal Quilt

Shapes, Problem Solving

Materials
- ✓ *Color Farm* by Lois Ehlert
- ✓ geometric shapes cut from paper (5 to 10 per student)
- ✓ 8" yellow paper squares (1 per student)
- ✓ 10" black paper squares (1 per student)
- ✓ glue
- ✓ paper punch
- ✓ yarn
- ✓ laminator or contact paper

Share Lois Ehlert's *Color Farm* with your students to inspire them to create their own farm animals from paper shapes. Encourage the students to experiment with the shapes to form the animals. When a child is satisfied with his picture, have him or her glue the shapes to a yellow paper square and write the animal's name on the picture.

Mount each picture on a black construction paper frame and laminate for durability. Ask a parent volunteer to punch holes around each picture and "sew" the squares together with yarn. Hang the paper quilt in the classroom for all to enjoy.

Mystery Animals

Critical Thinking, Writing

Give each child a sheet of light-colored construction paper. Instruct the class to fold the papers in half. Have each child think of a farm animal and write one clue about it on the front of the paper. (Ask an aide, a parent, or an older student to help your class with this part of the activity.) Then have the child open the paper and draw the animal inside. Have the student write the name of the animal beside its picture. When everyone has finished, let each child read his or her clue aloud while the rest of the class guesses the identity of the mystery animal.

Old MacDonald's Farm

Fine-Motor Skills, Music Appreciation

Give each child a copy of the farm animals pictured on page 90. Then instruct the children to color the animals and cut them out. Have them glue or tape a craft stick to the back of each animal. Then let the children hold up the appropriate animal puppet as they sing each verse of "Old MacDonald's Farm."

Variation:

Cut out the pictures of the farm animals and glue each one to a piece of paper. Place the pictures in a paper lunch bag. Then ask a student to reach in the bag and select an animal. Have the class identify the animal and use the animal's name to sing "Old MacDonald's Farm." Continue the procedure with other students.

Down by the Bay

Music Appreciation, Rhyming Words

Play the song "Down by the Bay" from *Playing Favorites* by Greg and Steve (Youngheart Music/Creative Teaching Press). Then ask the students to make up new verses that include farm animals. List the suggestions on the chalkboard or on chart paper. Here are some ideas your class will enjoy:

Did you ever see a cow kissing a sow . . .

Did you ever see a sheep taking a leap . . .

Did you ever see a goat sailing a boat . . .

Did you ever see a horse on a golf course . . .

Did you ever see a pig dancing a jig . . .

Sing the song with the new verses. Then write each line on a 12" x18" sheet of white paper, and let the students illustrate the new verses. Bind the pages together to make a "Down by the Bay" songbook.

Farm Animal Pancakes

Cooking

Materials

- ✓ pancake batter
- ✓ spoon
- ✓ griddle
- ✓ spatula
- ✓ measuring cup
- ✓ farm animal cookie cutters
- ✓ napkins or paper plates
- ✓ assorted toppings: raisins, small pieces of apple, candy pieces, chocolate chips, licorice, coconut, etc.

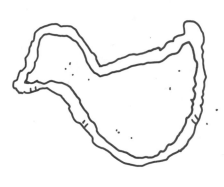

Help the students measure $\frac{1}{2}$ cup of batter at a time. Pour the batter onto the griddle and cook. When all the pancakes have been cooked, give one to each student. Have the students use farm animal cookie cutters to cut shapes from their pancakes. Let the students add various toppings to their animal creations. Eat and enjoy!

Food-Tasting Party

Culminating Activity

Materials

- ✓ a variety of food items that come from farm animals, such as hard-boiled eggs, cheese, yogurt, pudding, chicken nuggets, bite-sized portions of bacon and ham
- ✓ paper plates
- ✓ plastic forks and spoons

Host a festive food-tasting party as a culminating activity to your Farm Animals theme study. (Some parents may be able to contribute various food items for your students to try.) The children will be amazed at the many foods that come from farm animals!

Barn Pattern

89

Farm Animals

pig

goat

duck

hen

cow

sheep

horse

Dinosaurs

Take your students back in time to the days of the dinosaurs. Your students will be captivated as they study these fascinating creatures.

Exploration Corner

Transform your classroom into an environment in which dinosaurs would feel right at home! Here are some ideas for setting up an exciting Dinosaurs Exploration Corner.

🐾 Cut a six-foot-long dinosaur from butcher paper and tape it to the wall.

🐾 Cut large leaves from green paper and arrange them to look like ferns. Cut leaves and slender trunks to create palm trees. Tape the plants beside the dinosaur.

🐾 Stand a tall plant—either real or artificial—on the floor. Then make a large 3-dimensional dinosaur to stand beside it. Simply cut out two dinosaur shapes from colored butcher paper and staple the sides together, leaving an opening. Stuff the dinosaur with newspaper and staple shut. Add features with markers, and then place your dinosaur beside the plant.

🐾 Post an assortment of dinosaur posters and pictures on a bulletin board.

🐾 Display plastic or stuffed dinosaurs on a table or shelf. Arrange theme-related books beside them.

🐾 Set out dinosaur counters for your students to use for math activities.

Suggested Activities for the Exploration Corner

Add your own creative ideas to the activities suggested below:

🐾 Provide simple dinosaur shapes cut from paper. Tell your class that no one knows what colors dinosaurs were or what kinds of patterns (such as spots or stripes) were on their skin. Then have the students use their imagination and color or paint the dinosaurs any way they choose.

🐾 Set out playdough and let your students make miniature dinosaur models.

🐾 Put out a container of dinosaur counters. Invite the students to make a color pattern by arranging the dinosaurs in a line.

🐾 Set out a shallow box. Cover the bottom with sand. Have the children arrange plastic dinosaurs, artificial greenery, rocks, twigs, and other objects to make a scene of dinosaur days.

🐾 Provide theme-related dot-to-dot puzzles, mazes, and other activity sheets.

Books to Share

Here are some interesting books that will enrich your Dinosaur theme study.

Danny and the Dinosaur by Syd Hoff

Digging Up Dinosaurs by Aliki

The Dinosaur Alphabet Book by Jerry Pallotta

Dinosaur Bob by William Joyce

Dinosaur Chase by Carolyn Otto

Dinosaur Day by Liza Donnelly

Dinosaurs Dancing by Luella Connelly (Creative Teaching Press)

Dinosaurs, Dinosaurs by Byron Barton

Dinosaur Roar by Paul and Henrietta Stickland

The Enormous Egg by Oliver Butterworth

If the Dinosaurs Came Back by Bernard Most

The Magic School Bus in the Time of the Dinosaurs by Joanna Cole

Activities

Goal-Setting Chart

Record-Keeping, Organization

Show your class pictures of dinosaurs. Tell the students that dinosaurs lived millions of years ago and that what we know about them comes from discoveries that scientists have made. Then divide a sheet of chart paper into three columns and label them with the following headings: *What We Already Know, What We Want to Know, What We Learned.* Ask the students to state dinosaur facts they already know and write their responses in the first column. Next, ask what they would like to find out during their theme study. Write those ideas in the second column.

As the children work through this unit and find out interesting facts about dinosaurs, write those discoveries in the third column. At the end of the theme study, your students will be proud of how much they've learned!

Extension:

Reproduce a copy of the Dinosaurs multipurpose page (page 104), and record the information from the completed chart on it. Then reproduce the page for each child, and have the students take the papers home to share with their families.

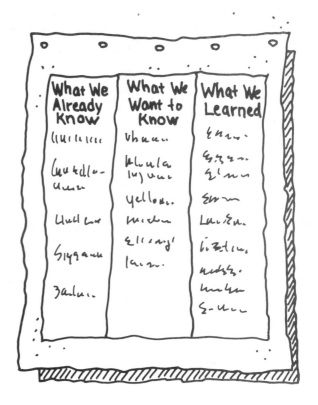

Dinosaur Scene

Art, Critical Thinking

Have your students look at dinosaur books to get an idea of what dinosaurs looked like. Then divide the class into small groups. Have each group paint a scene from dinosaur days. Encourage the students to show dinosaurs doing different activities, such as munching on leaves, caring for their young, or fighting their enemies. Afterwards, have the groups share their scenes with the class.

Dinosaur Booklets

Science

Give each child a copy of the dinosaurs pictured on page 103. Discuss the animals with the class. Share these facts:

- **Brachiosaurus** was one of the largest dinosaurs. It was as tall as a building. It was a plant eater.
- **Saltopus** was only as big as a cat. It was a meat eater. It could run fast.
- **Stegosaurus** was as big as an elephant. It was a plant eater. It had large bony plates on its back.
- **Triceratops** had three horns on its head. It used its horns to fight and protect itself. It was a plant eater.
- **Tyrannosaurus** was a meat eater. It had sharp teeth and powerful legs. People call it the "king of the dinosaurs" because it was so fierce.

Have the class color the pictures and cut them out. Give each child five 6" x 9" sheets of paper. Instruct the students to glue a dinosaur on each page and to add background scenery. Staple the pages together to make booklets for students to take home.

Extension:

Write a sentence about each dinosaur. Reproduce the sentences and cut them into strips. Give each child a set of five sentences, and have the students glue the strips beside the appropriate pictures in their booklets.

Meat Eaters and Plant Eaters

Classification

Divide a sheet of chart paper into two columns. Write *Meat Eaters* in the first column and *Plant Eaters* in the second. Then as you and the class discover various dinosaurs and learn what they ate, write the dinosaur names in the correct column.

Stand-up Dinosaurs

Fine-Motor Skills

Give each child a copy of the dinosaurs on page 103. Have the class color the animals and cut them out. Then cut toilet paper tubes in half, and give five pieces to each child. Have the students glue their dinosaurs onto the tubes so that they stand up. Let the students work in groups and use their stand-up dinosaurs for the following activities:

- make up a story about dinosaurs and use the pictures to act it out
- manipulate the dinosaurs to solve addition and subtraction problems
- arrange the dinosaurs in a line to make an interesting pattern, such as Triceratops, Brachiosaurus, Triceratops, Saltopus, Triceratops, Tyrannosaurus

Baby Dinosaurs

Critical Thinking, Fine-Motor Skills

Tell your class that dinosaurs hatched from eggs. Add that when the babies hatched, they looked a lot like their parents. If possible, show illustrations of dinosaur babies hatching from colorful books such as Steve Parker's *Dinosaurs and How They Lived* and Angela Wilkes's *The Big Book of Dinosaurs*.

Next, give each child two paper eggs that have been stapled one on top of the other as shown. Instruct the children to cut a jagged line near the bottom of the top egg (the cover). Then have each student draw a picture of a baby dinosaur on the other egg. (The students may make up their own dinosaurs or create a baby based on dinosaur pictures they've studied.) Tell the students to draw their pictures so that the dinosaurs are hidden from view when the cover is down. Afterwards, let the students share their baby dinosaurs by lifting the covers off their eggs to show who is "hatching."

I'm a Paleontologist!

Role-Playing

Materials

✓ *Digging Up Dinosaurs* by Aliki
✓ large pretzel twists
✓ tub of sand
✓ small plastic spoons or knives
✓ varying sizes of paintbrushes
✓ adult-sized white shirts or lab coats
✓ toothbrushes
✓ magnifying glass (optional)

Share *Digging Up Dinosaurs* to help your class learn about the job of a paleontologist. Then let your students discover their own "dinosaur bones." First, break several pretzels into two or three pieces each, and then bury them in sand. Invite two or three children at a time to put on a "lab coat" and search for the bones in the sand. Have the children use plastic spoons or knives to dig for the bones and toothbrushes to clean them. Remind the class to handle the pieces gently. Challenge the students to piece the pretzels back together. If you like, provide magnifying glasses to let the students examine the bones better.

Fossil Clues

Observation

Tell the class that fossils help scientists learn about dinosaurs. Explain that fossils are the remains of animals or plants that have hardened into rock over the years. Explain that by looking at fossils, scientists can figure out what dinosaurs looked like. Then do this simple activity to show how fossils reveal information.

Give every child a ball of modeling clay. Instruct the students to mold their ball into a flat, oval shape. Then provide items that will leave an impression in the clay, such as paper clips, buttons, rulers, pencils, and lids of glue sticks or small bottles. Have each student choose an item and press it into the clay to form an impression of the entire object or insert only part of it into the clay to make a set of tracks. Afterwards, have the class examine the "fossils" and guess which items made the impressions.

Dinosong

Music

Share a lively Dinosaur song with your students. First, print the letters *d -i- n-o-saur* on the chalkboard or make letter cards for the children to refer to as they sing. Then have the children sing the song to the tune of "Bingo." Encourage the class to clap out the rhythm or make up simple actions to the verses.

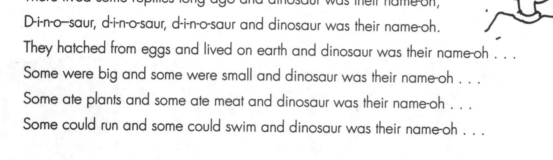

There lived some reptiles long ago and dinosaur was their name-oh,

D-i-n-o–saur, d-i-n-o-saur, d-i-n-o-saur and dinosaur was their name-oh.

They hatched from eggs and lived on earth and dinosaur was their name-oh . . .

Some were big and some were small and dinosaur was their name-oh . . .

Some ate plants and some ate meat and dinosaur was their name-oh . . .

Some could run and some could swim and dinosaur was their name-oh . . .

Have students expand the song by adding dinosaur facts they have learned.

Dinosaur Headbands

Art, Fine-Motor Skills

Let your students make dinosaur headbands and pretend they are dinosaurs! Give each student a copy of the Dinosaur Headband pattern on page 101. Instruct each child to color the dinosaur face and cut it out. Have the child cut out the two headband pieces. Then have the class follow the directions on the pattern page to complete the headbands. When all the headbands have been made, have the students wear them and walk around the classroom like dinosaurs. If you like, have the children sing the Dinosong (see the activity above) as they walk!

Dinosaur Roar

Oral Language, Movement

Share Paul and Henrietta Stickland's *Dinosaur Roar* with the class. List some of the key words or phrases on word cards and place them in a pocket chart. For example, you might use the following phrases:

dinosaur roar

dinosaur squeak

dinosaur fierce

dinosaur fast

dinosaur slow

dinosaur tiny

Read the story again and have the class chant the text with you. Point to the words in the pocket chart as you read. Then have the students stand up and do each action as you recite the text from the pocket chart.

Sentence Patterns

Reading

Write the following sentence: *Some dinosaurs were bigger than _____*. Reproduce the sentence so that each child gets a sentence strip. Have the students glue the strip to the bottom of a large sheet of drawing paper. Then instruct them to make pictures showing things smaller than a dinosaur, such as a person, an animal, or a car. Write the corresponding word in the blank space for each student. When all the pages are completed, bind them together to make a big book for the class. Add a construction paper cover that reads *Some dinosaurs were really big!* Your students will enjoy reading the book to each other.

Some dinosaurs were bigger than ____Trees____.

Pattern Block Dinosaurs

Problem Solving

Materials
- ✓ pattern blocks
- ✓ paper pattern blocks
- ✓ glue
- ✓ black construction paper

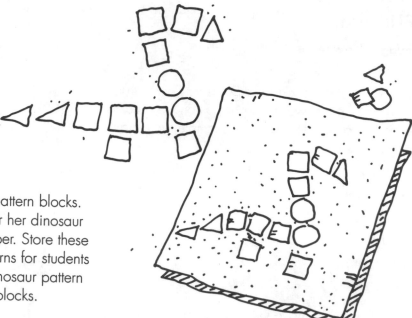

Have each student create a dinosaur with pattern blocks. Then have each child make a copy of his or her dinosaur by gluing paper pattern blocks to black paper. Store these paper dinosaurs in a basket or tray as patterns for students to copy. Simply let the students choose a dinosaur pattern and try to re-create the animal with pattern blocks.

Extensions:
- Have students count how many pattern blocks they used to make their dinosaurs. See who can use the smallest number of blocks.
- Have children graph the different blocks they used for their dinosaur pictures. Have them record which block they used the most and which one they used the least.

Dinosaur Art Gallery

Imaginative Thinking

Give each student a copy of the dinosaur pattern (page 102). Have the students color the patterns. After the students cut out their colored dinosaur shapes, have them draw facial features. Then have the children glue on paper features, such as horns, plates, spots, or stripes, to make their own unique dinosaurs. Display the dinosaurs to create a colorful art gallery in your classroom.

Dinosaur Headband Pattern

Color the dinosaur face. Cut it out.
Cut out the two pieces of the headband.
Put the headband together by matching
A to A, B to B, and C to C.

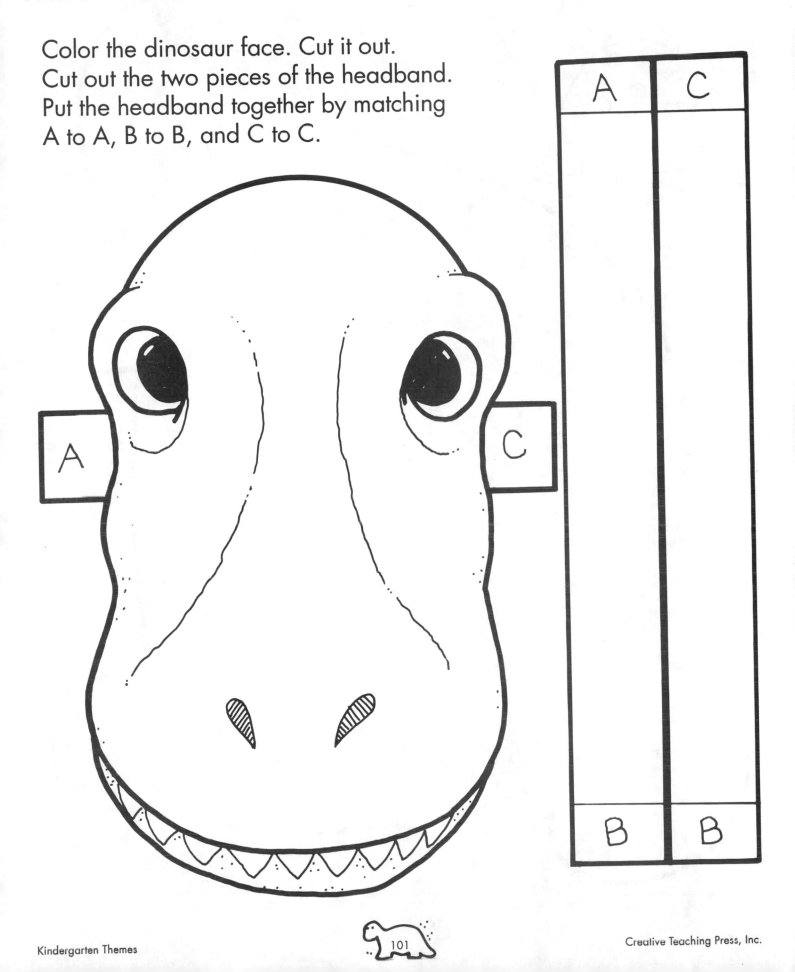

101

Dinosaur Pattern

Dinosaurs

Tyrannosaurus

Stegosaurus

Saltopus

Triceratops

Brachiosaurus